William Cullen Bryant
Updated Edition

Twayne's United States Authors Series

David J. Nordloh, Editor

Indiana University, Bloomington

TUSAS 59

Portrait of William Cullen Bryant by Henry Peters Gray.
Courtesy of the New-York Historical Society, New York.

William Cullen Bryant
Updated Edition

By Albert F. McLean

Point Park College

Twayne Publishers
A Division of G. K. Hall & Co. • *Boston*

William Cullen Bryant, Updated Edition
Albert F. McLean

Copyright 1989 by G. K. Hall & Co.
All rights reserved.
Published by Twayne Publishers
A Division of G. K. Hall & Co.
70 Lincoln Street
Boston, Massachusetts 02111

First edition © 1964, Twayne Publishers, Inc.

Copyediting supervised by Barbara Sutton
Book production by Janet Z. Reynolds
Book design by Barbara Anderson

Typeset in 11 pt. Garamond
by Modern Graphics, Inc., Weymouth, Massachusetts

Printed on permanent/durable acid-free paper
and bound in the United States of America

Library of Congress Cataloging-in-Publication Data

McLean, Albert F.
    William Cullen Bryant / by Albert F. McLean. — Updated ed.
        p.   cm. — (Twayne's United States authors series ; TUSAS 59)
    Bibliography: p.
    Includes index.
    ISBN 0-8057-7528-5 (alk. paper)
    1. Bryant, William Cullen, 1794–1878—Criticism and interpretation.
I. Title.   II. Series.
PS1181.M3 1989
811′.3—dc19   88–24713
                                                                          CIP

For Jean

Contents

About the Author

Albert F. McLean is Distinguished Professor of Humanities at Point Park College in Pittsburgh, where he teaches the history of American film, media criticism, and philosophy. For fifteen years he served as vice president and academic dean, until returning to teaching in 1987. In addition to this book on William Cullen Bryant, he has written a book on mass entertainment, *American Vaudeville as Ritual,* and an oral history of his college, *Point Park College: The First Twenty-five Years.*

McLean was educated at Williams College (Bryant's alma mater) and holds the doctoral degree in the History of American Civilization from Harvard University. Previous to taking a position at Point Park College, he taught at Tufts University and Transylvania University. He has published articles on Bryant, Melville, and Thoreau, as well as others on American vaudeville. He has been a contributor to *Notable American Women,* the *Dictionary of American Biography,* and the fourth edition of *The Oxford Companion to the Theatre.* A published poet, one of his nature poems having been included in the Borestone Mountain Awards volume, *Best Poems of 1960,* he contributed "William Cullen Bryant at the Tomb of Napolean Bonaparte" to the recent anthology *Under Open Sky: Poets on William Cullen Bryant.* He is currently working on a critical and historical study of nineteenth-century poetry.

Preface

In my preface to the first edition of this study of William Cullen Bryant I had asserted that the poet was "far different from the gentlemanly man-of-letters handed down to us by his nineteenth-century admirers." The book was, I claimed, an attempt to reveal "a drama of the inner life" and "find the deeper pulse of his life and art." From my vantage point two decades later, I can only admire the optimism of those lofty intentions. That very optimism served me well, however, and this book still contains, I find, useful insights into Bryant's work of poetic creation and the ends that he made it serve.

My view of Bryant today, however, has changed. My Bryant is not so much the young poet wrestling with his soul, his emotions and intellect in contention, cultivating the inward dynamics of the creative process. He is, rather, the adaptable Yankee who took the New York literary world, if not by storm, then by a healthy gale, a private man who pursued a course of self-education even into his advanced years, and a contemplative thinker who found that death was not the great problem that he had supposed, but was only the obverse of the love of life.

How full his life actually was, I had not been fully aware until the appearance of Charles H. Brown's weighty biography and the serial publication of the *Letters,* astutely edited and explicated by William Cullen Bryant II and Thomas G. Voss. Whereas my book had taken Bryant to task for not finding his poetic voice, I now recognize more clearly the place of his poetry in his complex life and how miraculous it was that he was able to pursue it as long and as far as he did. There is no reason for me to retract my views, for I still believe that his potential as a poet was much greater than he was able to realize. Given, however, the context provided by the biographical scholarship, it is apparent that his deficiencies as a poet, such as they were, are more than balanced by the sum of his life's work.

My appreciation of Bryant was also heightened and matured by the Centennial Conference in 1978, sponsored by the Center for Cultural and Intercultural Studies of Hofstra University. The range of topics addressed there, from horticulture to homeopathy, from urban planning to manifest destiny, from epistemology in literature to the eschatology of civil religion, is impressive in itself, quite aside from the high level of the papers. That Bryant was celebrated on the hundredth anniversary of his death is startling enough, but that so many scholars representing so many intellectual points of view found in his life and writings matters for serious consideration is more significant.

My preface to the first edition had wishfully asserted that the book contained "hints and directions for the creative spirits—readers as well as writers—of our day." The reappraisal of Bryant by "twenty present-day American poets" collected in *Under Open Sky* (1986) is a justification of my hopes, and I am still hopeful, perhaps even more so, for the years ahead. The awareness of the creative spirit and of our debts to the past is too easily obscured by mass culture and the troublesome events that impinge on our daily lives. But creativity flourishes in many forms today, and the mission of re-discovering its processes and history is, I believe, still valid and important.

This revised volume corrects points of error and omission in the original, a number of which were pointed out by people to whom I am indebted, but it also enlarges on topics that were insufficiently covered before, notably Bryant's hymns, his translations, his ac-counts of his travels, and the critical responses to his poetry by his contemporaries. While my interpretations of some of the poems has been modified to one degree or another, I decline to enter into a public debate with myself, and have let stand my original arguments with only minor emendations.

My renewed thanks to those who aided me in the preparation of the book in the sixties, and my additional appreciation to Gerhard Probst, who advised me regarding translation from the German.

Albert F. McLean

Point Park College, Pittsburgh

Chronology

1855 *Evening Post* supports Fremont and the Republican party.

1861 *Evening Post* supports Lincoln and the Union cause.

1864 *Thirty Poems* published.

1866 Frances Bryant dies.

1866–1867 Final voyage to Europe.

1870–1872 Translations of the *Iliad* and *Odyssey* published.

1878 Dies on 12 June. His estate, estimated at $1 million, is left to his two daughters, Fanny Bryant Godwin and Julia Sands Bryant. The *Evening Post* continues Bryant's policies under Parke Godwin's leadership.

Chapter One
A Poet's Life

To read the poetry of William Cullen Bryant is to engage in an act requiring both historical imagination and perceptive sympathy. If Bryant speaks to the twentieth century, he does so purely on his own terms. Though he created his poetry from the two sources from which all poets work—his heart and his experience—and though his honesty was bountifully rewarded in his own time, he seldom speaks to us of the matters most pertinent to our lives. Neither his remote personality nor his tendentious mind, neither the rural Yankee culture in which he developed nor the momentous national issues he debated in his maturity seem to be particularly significant when viewed from the perspective of our heavily urbanized, cosmopolitan existence.

To read Bryant today is to transcend the limits of contemporary taste and values and to participate vicariously in a creative experiment. To read this poet is to follow the intricate workings of the human imagination—seeking, selecting, contending with its raw materials—in the noble attempt to project a genuinely personal literature appropriate to a free and democratic culture. By restraining for the moment our quarrels with the past, we can possibly achieve some insight into the successes, as well as the failures, of the artistic sensibility as it took root and began to sprout on American soil.

In order to participate in this act of sympathetic understanding, we must discard the critical truisms that have relegated Bryant to the place of a dubious curiosity. The chaste and tidy envelope of the man of letters must be opened and its contents put on display. His poetry should be read for its own meaning and beauty without those furtive glances, typical of the academic eye, at the literary giants of other centuries and other cultures. And, in the light of the recent trend of Bryant scholarship, the ideas of the poems should be salvaged from the formalized and oversimplified patterns into which the intellectual historians have categorized them, and then they should be restored to their natural and designated context—

the texture of rhythmic and metaphorical language that is the poem itself.

There is no simple method by which Bryant, the poet-at-work, can be resurrected. This study deals with several facets of the central problem and, I hope, suggests and anticipates further exploration into the areas of the development of sensibility, theme, voice, and the assimilation of poetic creations by the culture at large. Primary to any understanding of the poems, of course, is an appreciation of the poet's aims, his interests, and his capacities. It is to this area that attention must first be directed.

Major Characteristics

For some time the major characteristics of Bryant's art have been an open secret. His seriousness, his simplicity, his moralism, his idealism, and his conscious craftsmanship have been the subjects of classroom discussions and scholarly articles for over fifty years. That he shared with the Enlightenment an admiration for the reasoning powers of the human mind and that he deplored both obscurity and emotional extravagances have long been apparent from his poetry and from his critical statements. Equally evident, however, is that he could write of the poet as one who, in the ecstasy of composition, should "Let thine own eyes o'erflow; Let thy lips quiver with the passionate thrill. . . ."[1] And, in poem after poem, Bryant perversely cultivated the qualities of mood in a manner that suggested more the romantic than the neoclassical poet. Thus, his profile—as it emerges from sophomore survey courses—is that of a "transitional poet" who somehow could not make up his mind whether to go backward or forward. Any gaps that may have occurred in explaining the man and his works have been conventionally stuffed with the caulking of Puritanism—which explains his moralism and his seriousness—and nationalism—sufficient to dispel doubts regarding his social idealism.

These are, of course, all partial truths appropriate to the occasions that called them forth. Bryant's poetry was preponderantly serious, simple, moralistic, idealistic, and skillfully constructed. He was familiar with the neoclassic temper, having read and composed in that vein during his youth; he responded early and powerfully to the message of the British romantics; and he later studied German, Spanish, and Portuguese verse. He had been familiar with New

England Calvinism in his youth, primarily through his mother's family, the Snells—that long line of worthy and earnest preachers. He had also shown an early interest in politics and, as a young man, become a vocal advocate of democracy and free trade. But all of this is to say merely that he was a clever, conscientious New Englander who, upon arriving in the metropolis of New York City, polished and exploited his talents in the best American fashion.

Bryant himself does not do much to correct this image of the successful, self-made poet. The only extant autobiography is fragmentary, breaking off at the very point where the Berkshire boyhood closes and the development of the mature man and artist begins. While this fragment contains hints as to the formation of basic attitudes, its substance is the vivid, charming story of family life in rustic New England. Bryant records the reading of the Bible at home; the stern Calvinism of his grandfather, Squire Snell; and the Federalist enthusiasms of his father, Dr. Peter Bryant. He tells of his own precocity (without any reference to his "genius"), and he also notes that he was, at one point, incapacitated by being kicked in the head by a horse. He remembers the corporal punishment, which supposedly developed the character of the young, and the pictures on the kitchen floor of the folk-lore Satan, "Old Crooktail." With ironic amusement he presents his earliest attempt at rhyming, a versification of the Book of Job: "His name was Job, evil he did eschew, To him were born seven sons; three daughters too."

Remarks that strike a somewhat deeper chord, and pertain more directly to the growth of the poet, are those that describe his adverse feelings toward the drunken militia, the quiet shock at his first sight of death at the funeral of a schoolmate, and his thoughtful observation of the religious "awakenings," which had spread—as they did through many rural counties in the early years of the nineteenth century—like an untamable conflagration over Cummington. Bryant recalls, more as observations upon his personal life than as contributing factors toward his poetry, his frequent poor health as a boy, the frustrations that arose from it, and also his early reading in his father's copious library. With half-concealed self-satisfaction, the mature Bryant looks back on his initial publication in the Hampshire *Gazette* of 1804 of a versification of the Hundred and Fourth Psalm, and, in 1809, of the pamphlet sponsored by his father, *The Embargo; Or Sketches of the Times, A Satire; by a Youth of Thirteen*.[2]

In the discussion of his college career, the attributes of character dominate almost entirely over those of sensitivity. In imitation of Sir William Jones, the self-made man whom he had admired in his youth, he extolled industry and fortitude in his remarks on his preparation for college—Greek and Latin under the demanding tutelage of his uncle, the Reverend Dr. Thomas Snell—and the ease with which he—young Bryant—had won recognition for his intellectual abilities at Williams College. Dissatisfied with the low level of instruction at Williams, however, he had made one of those mistakes that the successful man, compulsively it would seem, regrets all his life: he dropped out during his sophomore year and returned home in order to persuade his parents to support him at Yale College. Unable, or perhaps just unwilling, to bear the extra expense of Yale, his family refused to accommodate him. At this point, when he was seventeen, the autobiography makes note of the young man's reading in Southey, Kirke White, Cowper, Blair, and Bishop Porteus, but then it breaks off, leaving his audience to extrapolate, as it were, from the minor achievements to the major ones.[3]

In his eighties, Bryant wrote a poem titled "A Lifetime," in which the chronicle of his life is presented as a series of vignettes.[4] More like the pen-and-ink sketches in a Victorian novel than an honest assessment of times past, the verses describe the boyhood romps in the field; the attentive listening to Bible stories being read aloud in the evening; the young lawyer pleading his case before the bar; the domestic bliss of husband and father; the strenuous labors of the editor; the wanderings of the traveler in foreign lands; and the eventual old man, white-haired and grief-stricken, who stands over the graves of his wife and daughter.

No, William Cullen Bryant was understandably reticent about the creative life that lies buried under these commonplaces. After all, his struggles with his demon were recorded in his poetry. What the public eye needed, to give balance and justice to the picture, were not meditations on the inward self but the thread by which the common humanity of the poet could be unraveled. These superficial portraits were the clothes in which the naked poet could appear in public, tokens of his respect for the prosaic courses of ordinary lives. Only thus can these trivia be reconciled with the sharp intellect and passionate individualism of Bryant, the poet.

For, like the saint, the poet must live two lives: the one by which others know him; the other by which he knows himself.

Bryant's career with the *Evening Post* for fifty-two years, first as an associate editor and subsequently as proprietor and editor-in-chief, provides a notable instance of his willingness to merge into a stereotyped—in this case a corporate—personality. His own account of the critical years of his career was written and published in 1851 under the title of "Reminiscences of the *Evening Post.*"[5] Unlike the memoirs of two other publishers, Ben Franklin and Edward Bok, this reminiscence is less concerned with personalities than with policy. As Bryant shapes the image of the *Post* he edited, we identify, to be sure, the man with the institution. The liberal temper—in the style of Cobden and Bright—is Bryant's own political view. The ideological warfare which the *Post* had waged for two decades, and was to continue to wage, on the side of reform, progress, justice, and human freedom, was Bryant's personal war also. Yet the account which Bryant preferred to record was not that of his own contention with men and issues, but the story of the rise of the enlightened and responsible metropolitan dailies.

From Allan Nevins' comprehensive book, *The Evening Post: A Century of Journalism,* comes a sharper picture of Bryant in his editorial role. According to Nevins, Bryant was a bulwark of calm strength and conviction: "The foundation of Bryant's power as an editor lay simply in his soundness of judgment and his unwavering courage in maintaining it."[6] Faced with innumerable issues of every size and dimension—the tariff, Jackson's attack on the national bank, the Mexican War, imperialism, penal reform, the rights of labor, internal improvements, international copyright, freedom of the press, stabilization of the currency—Bryant and the *Post* maintained a critical alertness and perseverance that commended itself to a large following.

Professor Nevins also makes the point that the *Post* was a paper with principles: "Freedom and democracy—to these two principles every utterance of the *Evening Post* in its fifty years under Bryant was referred. Other journals might think of the day only and let the morrow take care of itself, but he was solicitous that each issue should fit into the exposition of a policy good for the year and the decade."[7] Nevertheless, influential as these principles of freedom and democracy may have been, Bryant and the *Post* carefully refrained from systematically defining them, or from making any broader application of them than the events of the day warranted. As Godwin (associate editor under Bryant and successor to the editorship) noted, Bryant stopped far short of doctrinaire commitments. His consistency, it would seem, was more pragmatic than absolute. If the fruit of his judgment was freely articulated for public consumption, the roots of his principles remained buried deep within.

The social image of the man does not lead us very far into his creative center. His friendships were many and various; but close companions, outside of his family, were rare. His eulogies on Cooper, Irving, and Verplank reveal only a slight personal warmth for these men with whom he had associated; and his poems to William Leggett, John Lothrop Motley, and Thomas Cole[8] were distinguished for their lofty and abstract praise of public virtues. He appears to have lacked that appeal and social charm characteristic of many of the nineteenth-century men of letters and to have made little effort to win friends or readers through the application of personal warmth. A magazine writer of the early 1830s expressed a prevailing view of Bryant when he noted that "His manners are quiet and unassuming, and marked with a slight dash of diffidence; and his conversation (when he does converse, for he is more used to thinking than talking), is remarkably free from pretension, and is characterized by good sense rather than genius."[9]

Parke Godwin, associate editor of the *Post* and the son-in-law and biographer of Bryant, confirms this impression while seeing deeper into the man. Godwin observed that the action of Bryant's eyes was the key to his presence and that his voice was his best recommendation in social intercourse. This is how Godwin described his first meeting with the poet in 1832:

He was of middle age and medium height, spare in figure, with a clean-shaven face, unusually large head, bright eyes, and a wearied, severe, almost saturnine expression of countenance. One, however, remarked at once the exceeding gentleness of his manner, and a rare sweetness in the tone of his voice, as well as an extraordinary purity in his selection and pronunciation of English. His conversation was easy, but not fluent, and he had the habit of looking the person he addressed so directly in the eyes that it was not a little embarrassing at first. A certain air of abstractedness in his face made you set him down as a scholar whose thoughts were wandering away to his books; and yet the deep lines about the mouth told of struggle either with himself or with the world.[10]

Nearly thirty years later, Nathaniel Hawthorne, who was himself known for his quietness and reserve, was to remark on the qualities of Bryant's eyes, finding them "keen eyes, without much softness in them." And his assessment of his visitor bears out that of Godwin: "[Bryant] was not in the least degree excited about [the suffering of Charles Sumner] or any other subject. He uttered neither passion nor poetry, but excellent good sense, and accurate information, on whatever subject transpired; a very pleasant man to associate with, but rather cold, I should imagine, if one should seek to touch his heart with one's own. He shook hands kindly all round, but not with any warmth of gripe [*sic*], although the ease of his deportment had put all on sociable terms with him."[11]

Perhaps this remoteness in Bryant's bearing is responsible for the scarcity of friendly comment by his contemporaries upon his art. Certainly his personal correspondence, even with his intimates, supplies little insight into his working method or his creative goals. When Bryant corresponded about his poetry, his remarks generally pertained to publication arrangements and to critical response. Even toward Edward T. Channing, who, as editor of the *North American Review,* bore a major responsibility for Bryant's emergence as a national poet, Bryant maintained a cordial but diffident relationship in correspondence. In 1819, upon being pressed by Channing for more material, Bryant replied in an overly modest manner, almost to the point of archness: "I may perhaps, some time or other, venture a little collection of poetry in print,—for I do not write much— and should it be favorably received, it may give me courage to do something more."[12]

Collect them he did, two years later in *Poems,* and roughly each decade throughout his life. *Poems* was updated in 1832, *The Fountain and Other Poems* appeared in 1842, and then followed *The White-Footed Deer and Other Poems* (1846), *Thirty Poems* (1864), and finally, a nearly complete collection two years before his death, *The Poetical Works of William Cullen Bryant* (1876). Yet lacking in all of these collections is a formulated intention or principle of selection. Bryant gave his readers no caption (or useful introduction) to lead into the heart of his verse, such as we find, of course, in *Leaves of Grass, Children of the Night,* and *North of Boston.* Cast like commodities upon the market, it is not surprising that Bryant's poems should be accepted as the products of an entirely reputable but unknowable manufacturer.

In "The Poet" Bryant recognized the desirability of the artist concealing himself behind his work. Here, after all, was the source of the "witchery" of art. The wonder and admiration of the reader are, these lines imply, best evoked by processes of which he is unaware. Like Hawthorne, who had compared the romancer to the weaver who works out the intricate patterns of his tapestry from the reverse side, Bryant saw that the secrets of the poet's craft were the more effectual for being somewhat mysterious. "The Poet," having hinted at these secrets and their source ("impassioned thought"), concludes with the highest tribute the adoring public can bestow upon a poet:

> "What witchery hangs upon this poet's page!
> What art is his the written spells to find
> That sway from mood to mood the willing mind!"[13]

The Expanding Sensibility

To reconstruct the sensibility of a poet who consistently shielded himself behind the social masks of his day, who treasured the privacy of his gift, and who appeared at many times not to recognize his own genius, is a task best undertaken through an examination of the poems themselves. Yet each poem seeks its context within a lifelong development of the artist, a development that has its own laws and its own prerogatives. Such as it is, no series of generalizations can infallibly delineate the maturing processes of a sensibility; no pattern imposed upon it can explain its vagaries or its inconsistencies. At best, the phases through which it passes can be distinguished and the leading tendencies remarked.

Among all the theorists of sensibility, Emerson best understood its volatile nature and respected its organic quality. When, in the essay "Circles," he described the life of man as "a self-evolving circle, which, from a ring imperceptibly small, rushes on all sides outward to new and larger circles," he marked that special quality that the poet, above ordinary men, cultivates. Particularly is this true of the poet who writes in an open society that is relatively free from the taboos and rituals of tradition and who thinks, feels, and writes from his own immediate experience. The phases of his development shape themselves as concentric circles. For Bryant, as for many other American poets, the career in art was—as Emerson described it—"an apprenticeship to the truth that around every circle another can be drawn."[14]

What are the perceptible circles of Bryant's expanding sensibility? Five suggest themselves most clearly, and they should suffice for this study. The inner circle is that of the precocious young Bryant as he discovered the mysteries of language; the second, that of the young man (college student and barrister) who learns the quality of his peculiar vision; the third, the circle of intellectual awakening, in which ideas become immediate and distinct; the fourth, the phase that begins in his middle thirties in which he yearns for broader and more encompassing areas of experience, in which he travels, reads, and translates; the fifth, the outer circle, which may be named the circle of wisdom. Within this organic paradigm each of Bryant's poems falls into place and finds its proper relevance. Within it, we can relate, with some assurance, the inner man to his work.

The "imperceptibly small" circle at the center of Bryant's sensibility was that nurtured by the close family life at Cummington and Hampshire. Each of his parents left an indelible impression upon his sensibility, as did the years of schooling in the classics, the proximity of rich and abundant nature, and the back-country religious orthodoxy. But his parents, especially, were foremost in his memory when he sat down many decades later to recount the days of his boyhood. His father was an intellectual and sophisticated man of the world who practiced medicine, read the classics, played the violin, and reveled in the political activity that took him often to Boston. His mother was devoutly religious, very close to her family and the land they had inhabited for several generations, attentive to her children, ambitious for them and for her husband. Most of all, both were parents who were talkers and writers— articulate persons who brought into the home the books and the visitors that would challenge the mind and the ear of any sensitive boy.

The poet, looking back on his childhood, attributed his early reading—the Bible at the age of four—to his mother's influence. He conjectures that "finding me rather docile, [Sarah Bryant] took pleasure in bringing me forward somewhat prematurely." He recalls also that she was, as was customary for pious New Englanders from the earliest days of settlement, a conscientious diarist who briefly noted each day the neighborhood gossip and her "simple occupations."[15] Through his mother's piety, most importantly, young

Cullen was wrapped in the language of religious worship, its rhythms, its images, and its rhetorical structures. From his third year the boy attended church regularly, listened to the long sermons and the readings from Scripture, and sang the regular, rhymed hymns from the traditional Watt's *Hymnal*. And, lest the soul should lapse from grace, in the household of Squire Snell there were the evening and morning prayers, which Cullen, during his visits, attended. The Calvinist theology passed by the boy, but the language did not. Remembering the particular beauty of some of these occasions of worship, Bryant described those who conducted the services as being "often poets in their extemporaneous prayers":

I have often, in my youth, heard from them prayers which were poems from beginning to end, mostly made up of sentences from the Old Testament writers. How often have I heard the supplication, "Let thy church arise and shine forth, fair as the moon, clear as the sun, beautiful as Tirzah, comely as Jerusalem, and terrible as an army with banners." One expression often in use was peculiarly impressive, and forcibly affected by childish imagination. "Let not our feet stumble on the dark mountains of eternal death." Then there was that prayer for revolution, handed down probably from the time of the Roundheads. "And wilt thou turn, and turn, and overturn, till he shall come whose right it is to reign, King of Nations, as of now King of Saints."[16]

For the poet who was to conceive and execute "Thanatopsis" these lofty phrases, the dignified but uncomplicated diction, and the rolling rhetoric were a profound influence. What had survived of the colonial "plain style" in which the Puritan clergymen had composed their sermons was to find its further extension in Bryant's blank verse, even though the promise of salvation concerned him little.

Through Dr. Peter Bryant, however, Cullen became familiar with language on a different level. No mere handmaid to Protestant piety, the language his father enjoyed was that of rational conversation, the play of wit, and the delightful and delicate harmonies the classical poets had cultivated. The dull exercises of Latin and Greek in the schoolroom became the vehicles of beauty and wonder when his father recited passages from the ancients. The crabbed grammar and syntax thrust upon the student by his uncle, the Reverend Snell, became the weapons of the imagination and intellect when the good doctor directed his son to translate the third book of the *Aeneid*. At sixteen the boy responded to Virgil's forceful, melodic description of the tempest with a translation that reveals his well-developed sensitivity to verbs, to the interrupted line, and to the trisyllabic foot:

> While thus he mourns a roaring tempest strides,
> Fierce from the north, and rends its vessels sides,
> Tremendous surges, rising from the main,
> Aloft to heaven the labouring bark sustain,
> Its oars are shattered, and the waters ride.
> (Its prow inverted,) dashing on its side. [17]

But even earlier he had tested his métier and discovered the uses of wit in crude satires and lampoons. At twelve and thirteen he had written pastorals in the manner of the Augustan poets, including an "Ode to the Connecticut River." Absorbed in the magical play of assonance and alliteration, he gave voice to such experimental lines as these from "The Spring Walk":

> Again the vivid green I tread
> With garments fluttering in the gale;
> Or stretched beneath the deepening shade,
> The balmy breath of Spring inhale . . . [18]

Dr. Bryant had encouraged the boy in this direction, as well as toward the creation of the extended poem, "The Embargo"; but he also lent a sharply critical ear to the young poet's attempts at verse. On one occasion Cullen, anticipating his father's praise, brought him an elegy beginning with the lines, "The word is given, the cruel arrow flies/With death-foreboding aim, and Woodbridge dies." [19] The young poet was shocked, however, to learn "that it was nothing but tinsel and would not do." Thus, language—as it was subjected to the craft of the poet and exploited for its aesthetic values—became, through this remarkable father, the poet's first and most valuable resource.

The Circle of Vision

Although his interest in and aptitude for language was to continue to grow, it ceased to dominate his poetry after his seventeenth year. By then he had entered fully his second circle and had begun to develop that faculty of vision that marks his mature verse. Vision is, of course, more than the sensory act of seeing; but it begins with the moment of conscious perception. Both his walks through the wooded countryside and his studies in botany had fastened upon him the habits of close observation, and it was from these visual experiences, impressed upon the mind sharply and in detail, that a number of his best poems were to be created. If the act of perception in itself had not carried its own authority, then Bryant's reading in the eighteenth-century philosophical psychologists Thomas Reid and Dugald Stewart,[20] who stressed the role of sensory perception in the acquisition of knowledge, would have brought the significance of his seeing before him. More and more, as he left behind him the bookish imagery and the fanciful scenery of the classical poets, he incorporated his own observation into his poems. Both his boyhood curiosity and psychological studies converged in the formation of a predominantly visual poetry. From 1818 to 1822 the bulk of his published poems, which were drawn from the visual experiences of his New England rambles, communicated the joy of discovering this second circle of sensibility. "The Yellow Violet" (1814, 1821), "To a Waterfowl" (1815, 1818), and "A Walk at Sunset" (1821), are all magnificent achievements of this type.

    While the vision Bryant cultivated during these years was partially the pure sensory experience—the recording of images upon the tabula rasa of the mind—it was also a creative act, engaging not merely the senses but the whole personality of the poet. The doctrine of the "association of ideas," as he had come across it in his reading, gave a plausible account of the way in which the mind, upon receiving sensory stimuli, associates them with experiences from the past. Wordsworth had responded to this psychology of association, and Bryant would seem to have read the *Lyrical Ballads* with growing interest from 1815 to 1820.

    From Wordsworth, as well as from the theorists of the British school, the essential point was easily discovered: vision consisted not merely of the natural object directly perceived but also of the entire complex of feeling and thought that simultaneously arose in the poet. Thus, the phenomena observed on the long strolls took on fascinating new dimensions as the poet exercised his newfound capacity. By 1821 he had become adept in responding to nature in this way. The vision of the sunset in "A Walk at Sunset" was not merely of the "thousand trembling lights" but also of the "bright isles beneath the setting sun"—the realms of death of which Indian lore had spoken. "The Rivulet" was not only a visible sign of nature's carefree joy; it is also a reminder of the poet's lost youth—and the lost youth of the entire "fading race of men." Similarly, "The West Wind" becomes a symbol for the persistent melancholy of man, even in the midst of nature's beauty.

Melancholy, in fact, is an almost inevitable product of the associationism in which Bryant engaged. The modern mind, alerted to the mysterious correlations between childhood and psychic disturbance, cannot help noting the constant recurrence of feelings of regret and guilt that are set loose by the process of memory. The guilt feelings occasionally emerge, as in "The Yellow Violet," but more often they are just beneath the surface, a shadow beneath the polished ice of the perfected verses. The themes of Bryant's poems tell us more than the passages in which explicit and rational thought is given its say; and these themes are predominantly those of death, loneliness, humility, and the passing of innocence. The association of ideas, set in motion by the act of seeing, is the process by which Bryant came to terms with the hidden core of his emotional life. The source of his anxieties remained obscure and repressed, but in such passages as the following (the italics are mine) we can observe how powerfully the simple act of seeing became for him a vehicle of intense and dark emotions:

About this time [1809] occurred an event which I remember with regret. My grandfather Snell had always been substantially kind to me, and ready to forward any plan for my education, but when I did what in his judgment was wrong, he reprimanded me with a harshness which was not so well judged as it was probably deserved. I had committed some foolish blunder, and he was chiding me with even more than his usual severity; I turned and looked at him with a steady gaze. "What are you staring at?" he asked. "Did you never see me before?" *"Yes,"* I answered: *"I have seen you many times before."* He never before had heard a disrespectful word from my lips. He turned and moved away . . . .[21]

This steady gaze Godwin had found disconcerting upon first meeting Bryant, and the same expression is recorded in the portrait in oils by Samuel F. B. Morse. While the eyes look outward toward Grandfather Snell, journalists, and people at large, they also look inward, framing the immediate perception within the totality of the poet's experience. The words of impudence to his grandfather were half involuntary, expressing the kind of response to the moment better left to poetry. Henceforth the poet would, in social intercourse, remain mute behind this gaze, leaving to the sensible man of affairs whom society had molded the business of maintaining human relations.

"To a Waterfowl" belongs to the outward circumference of the circle of vision.[22] In this poem, patently inspired by the personal observation of a wild bird at evening, perception evolves into an intricately structured response to experience. The eye, prompted by emotional conflicts of which the mind is only half-conscious, turns inward, then outward once more—relating, mediating, resolving. The image of the bird becomes symbolic of the man who is also flying into the blinding darkness; who is, like the bird, dimly aware of the fowlers that stalk him; and who is also familiar with the immensity of the physical world. But deeper, at the core of the poem, and closer to the crux of the poet's disturbance, is the other symbol: that of the fowl's "solitary way" that is also the poet's "long way that I must tread alone."

The poem is really about the "way" of the lonely, isolated individual; and its entire structure forms itself about the poet's sense of motion through time and space. Each stanza of the poem deals intensely with one or another aspect of the "way"; each major shift in the development of the theme offers a new perspective upon the "way." Thus, the impact of the sensory impression upon the imagination of the artist is not fragmented and momentary but is distended through time until the mind sees not only the bird in flight but the continuous flight of the bird. In "To a Waterfowl" all of the qualities of Bryant's vision are both fully realized and skillfully integrated:

> Whither, midst falling dew,
> While glow the heavens with the last steps of day,
> Far, through their rosy depths, dost thou pursue
> Thy solitary way?
>
> Vainly the fowler's eye
> Might mark thy distant flight to do thee wrong,
> As, darkly seen against the crimson sky,
> Thy figure floats along.
>
> Seek'st thou the plashy brink

Of weedy lake, or marge of river wide,
Or where the rocking billows rise and sink
On the chafed ocean-side?

There is a Power whose care
Teaches thy way along that pathless coast—
The desert and illimitable air—
Lone wandering, but not lost.

All day thy wings have fanned,
At that far height, the cold, thin atmosphere,
Yet stoop not, weary, to the welcome land,
Though the dark night is near.

And soon that toil shall end;
Soon shalt thou find a summer home, and rest,
And scream among thy fellows; reeds shall bend,
Soon, o'er thy sheltered nest.

Thou'rt gone, the abyss of heaven
Hath swallowed up thy form; yet, on my heart
Deeply has sunk the lesson thou hast given,
And shall not soon depart.

He who, from zone to zone,
Guides through the boundless sky thy certain flight,
In the long way that I must tread alone,
Will lead my steps aright.

(cited in full)

If "To a Waterfowl" is primarily a poem of vision, it also antic-ipates the next phase of Bryant's development as an artist. Only slightly submerged beneath the surface are the intellectual issues which many of his subsequent poems probe. There is, first, the questioning posture which always falls just short of agnosticism. There is, second, the belief in the God of Nature, the "Power whose care/Teaches thy way." Whether or not this deity, responsible for the instinctive workings of animate nature, is also a personal god, the patron of mankind, and the upholder of a moral order is a perennial problem in the poems of nature. Third, there is the question of the internal division within man—the contention for su-premacy between the reason and the heart.

These problems are resolved through the process of the poem. The fourth and eighth stanzas with their "Power whose care / Teaches thy way" and "He who, from zone to zone / Guides . . ." are not pious platitudes; they are efforts of the mind, and then the heart, to relate within the context of this particular experience past certainties to present doubts. As Richard Wilbur perceived, "It is a poem which opens with a question—which inquires as well as asserts or teaches. One of its strengths is that it implicitly admits the possibility of lostness and unbelief; it proceeds from rosy light to darkness, from the known to the unknown; there are sinister overtones in such words as 'solitary,' 'desert,' and 'abyss.' All of this keeps the poem honest and strengthens its affirmation."[23] This honesty of which Wilbur speaks is not the product of leisurely speculation on religious problems. It comes from the truth of a single experience, of a vision of sorts. Bryant's vision, however, was dissimilar to that of a seer or mystic who improvises epiphanies in unlikely places; his was the vision of discovery, the bringing to light of the mysterious truths of a man alive in the natural order.

The capacity to "see" continued to develop within the poet. By 1825, in the *Lectures on Poetry,* he was to speak confidently of the "correspondences" and "analogies" of poetry and, by implication, to recognize their centrality in his own work. He found in the landscapes of the Hudson River School painters, notably Thomas Cole, a visual and emotional equivalent of his own work. It was most significant that the painting by Asher B. Durand in 1849 of Cole and Bryant standing together on a rocky promontory in the Catskills, surrounded by underbrush and foliage, was titled "Kindred Spirits."

The Further Circles

But beyond the circle of vision was the great circle of ideas. The poet had, of course, made tentative contact with the intellectual life early, and "The Embargo" had, to some extent, shown his speculative mentality. "Thanatopsis" is notable for its sage reasoning and for its neat argumentation. The real and the continuing enthusiasm for abstract thought, however, does not manifest itself until the poet has perfected his vision and has made contact with the heterogeneous cultures of Cambridge and New York City. The imagination of the poet, once secure in its operations, could assimilate the issues presented to it by the world.

The first of the great issues to engage the poet was that of death; the second, that of human progress. Each issue developed in its own way, at its own rate; and subsequent chapters of this study will deal with the place within the poet's work of these momentous themes. The poems of death, which fed upon the images supplied by the "graveyard poets," came to terms with the conflicting religious and scientific ideologies of the day, and in them the poet discovered a truly personal synthesis of vision and idea. The poems of progress drew heavily upon the political convictions of Bryant's liberal associates—Catherine and Theodore Sedgewick, John Bigelow, William Leggett—yet sought their meaning not in particular events, parties and programs, but in the broader perspective of the natural order of the universe.

In both the poems of death and the poems of progress there are, from work to work, the signs of resoluteness and of vacillation, of a great and compelling lucidity and of a sluggish banality, of a remarkable eagerness and of a melancholy resignation. There is no single attitude or idea which describes the body of poems dealing with either of these themes; there are only high points and low pints, discoveries and evasions. For reasons that this study will explain in detail, the poems of death reached their apex quickly in "Thanatopsis" (1821), but the poems of progress postponed their full realization until their appearance in "The Fountain" (1839) and "The Antiquity of Freedom" (1842).

But both kinds of poems represent years of contemplation and experimentation. Each poem is a hypothesis to be confirmed in the crucible of the creative process. Each fresh insight has been measured by the ear, by the eye, and by the heart. In a sense these poems are synthetic, depending not upon their conceptual consistency alone but upon many elements of structure, metrics, and imagery. In a sense, also, there are no successes or failures among them, for each should be judged in terms of its contribution to the total expansion of the circle of ideas.

There are other ideas, of course, in Bryant's work. One can single out the themes of power, of innocence, of beauty, or of despair. All of these find their expression early in his career and reappear from time to time in varying configurations. As his vision took form, Bryant increased his capacity for reflection, and the crude statements of the intellectual novice are refined into the pure art of the major poems. Even the less sophisticated poems have their interest, for they often reveal the poet at work; he is attempting to break through his limitations and reach out toward fuller realization of his themes.

This outward thrust led him, over the years, to the broader circle of his maturity. About 1830 a new and different stability and firmness appear in his poems, and we find the ambitious young poet from the provinces responding to the richer, subtler culture of the city. The quality of mind is finer, less argumentative and more persuasive in such poems as "The Evening Wind" (1829), "To Cole, The Painter, Departing for Europe" (1829), "To the Fringed Gentian" (1832), and "The Prairies" (1832). His initial discovery of ideas had led him into overstatement; but—with time and experience behind him, with his place among the leaders of the American literary life secure, and with the stimulating prospect of new faces to see, new places to go, new ambitions to fulfill—his attitudes become less strained and his tone less extravagant. Over the years his maturity tended to become characterized by mellowness and relaxation, but the period beginning around 1830 and extending into the 1840s is one of vital and strenuous exploration.

To this period belongs his developing fascination with the wider horizons of the literature of other languages and a consequent urge to travel to other countries. As a youth he had been familiar with other cultures from his reading in the classical literatures in Greek and Latin, and upon taking up residence in New York City he developed friendships with people speaking both French and Spanish. Under their tutelage he acquired sufficient mastery of their languages to read and translate poetry in both. Subsequently he became familiar—how adept is not clear—with German and Italian and was reputed to have learned Portuguese and modern Greek. While his translations from the French and Spanish were initiated before traveling abroad, his translations of German poetry began with his periods of residence in Munich and Heidelberg in 1834.

Bryant may well have been predisposed to German literary subject matter, for he frequently experimented with folk themes and ballads characteristic of European romanticism. Applying the idealization of folk expression as Schiller had formulated in his *Naive and Sentimental Poetry,* Bryant had composed "The Song of Marion's Men" (1831), "Catterskill Falls" (1836), and "The White-Footed Deer" (1843). While actually residing in Germany, he composed "The Strange Lady" (1835) and "The Hunter's Vision" (1835). Two other poems have close similarities to ballads by Goethe: "The Hunter's Vision" (1835) closely resembles *"Der Fischer,"* and "A Presentiment" (1837) depicts the fatal ride of the father and his bewitched son of Goethe's *"Erlkönig."*[24] Bryant's ephemeral fiction, written on assignment for the "gift books" of the era, were Gothic tales of the mysterious and supernatural, a genre that looked back to German literature of the late eighteenth century even while seeking relevance to the American experience.[25]

Whether the boy from the Berkshires became a true cosmopolite is open to question, but the expansion of his horizon kept him alive as a poet and established him—along with Washington Irving, James Fenimore Cooper, and Henry Wadsworth Longfellow—as a champion of a broader, more humane culture. Characteristically, he was diffident about his intentions, but he read and traveled as his curiosity prompted him. There is no sense that his personality or interests made a radical shift, but then he had never been provincial in his attitudes. Rather, there seems to have been a process of assimilation as novel ideas and fresh material for poetry challenged him.

The accounts of his inveterate travels (five trips across the Atlantic and others to Latin America) were not the systematic and complete records of, say, a Bayard Taylor, but appeared sporadically in the *Evening Post*. They were later revised and collected in two volumes, *Letters of a Traveler* (1850, 1859) and *Letters from the East* (1869). One finds in these "letters" detailed descriptions of the folk ways and daily lives of the people he observed, enthusiastic passages on scenery, scattered complaints about the hazards of travel, and impressions, sometimes little more than gossip, about local politics. There are some brief portraits of picturesque characters encountered, stories told to him by natives, critiques of painting and architecture, and other such miscellany. His personal preoccupations surface periodically, and thus the readers of the *Evening Post* would learn about funeral rites, graveyards, lunatic asylums and horticulture.

Notably lacking, however, are accounts that might be expected of his meetings with the literary elite of these countries or with American travelers. (Hawthorne gives a full account of his meeting with Bryant, but Bryant neglects, in his *Letters,* to mention meeting Hawthorne and even passes vaguely over his own encounter with Wordsworth.) If one were unfamiliar with his poetry, it could be

easily inferred from the letters that he was not only unfamiliar with
the literary culture of these countries but had little interest in that
of the United States.

Reserved for a small portion of his poetry was the imaginative
invasion of foreign ways so neglected by the journalist. One can
turn to "Earth" (1835), "The Knight's Epitaph" (1835), "To the
Apennines" (1836), and "The Child's Funeral" (1835) for his perceptive responses to Italy. For his reactions to Germany there are
his translations of Uhland and his elegy "The Death of Schiller"
(1838). He translated Spanish poetry prior to his visit to Spain, but
"The Ruins of Italica" (1857), from the poetry of Rioja, was prompted
by his own tour of the ruins of Italica during his first trip to Spain.
It is difficult to pinpoint, however, any poems, or translations,
which can be directly attributed to his travel experiences in England,
Scotland, France, or the Near East. It would seem that all too often
the "witchery" of the poet was suppressed in the American tourist.

Had Emerson developed to its ultimate conclusion his figure of
concentric circles as they appear either in the pool or in vision, he
would have noticed that the ultimate circle not only approaches the
universality of nature itself but also is a dissipation of strength and
a blurring of vision. This is the paradox of Bryant's later poems: in
their wisdom they lack the power that is generated by polarity and
conflict. From the late 1840s, the pressure of the steady gaze di-
minishes. Although the command of verse technique persists and
although the poet continues to bring image to idea and idea to
image, the poems themselves are too easy to paraphrase, too quick
to declare themselves, too sure of their tone and mood. By the time
that Bryant was to compose "The Poet," he had long since passed
the time when he wrote under the stimulus of deeply felt emotion.
In "The Old Man's Counsel" (1840) he predicts the failure of his
vision, and in "Among the Trees" (1868) he betrays his inability
to respond to the living forces in nature.

Moments of conviction and new insights into the problems that
had concerned him in his youth restored from time to time within
his later years some of the former creativity, and, as a subsequent
chapter will demonstrate, poems such as "The Death of Lincoln,"
"The Death of Slavery," and especially "October, 1866" have their
own kind of effectiveness. There are also some remarkable lines and
passages in poems that are otherwise weak. Bryant cannot be said,
therefore, to have undergone the total decline that characterizes the

careers of many American artists. The creative process, in becoming habitual, may have lost its sense of urgency, and, in spite of its willingness to adventure, it may have quickly reached its limitations—but the impulse was still there.

In reverting once more to the translation of foreign poets in his waning years, it was not to the works of the lyrical romanticism that he turned, but back to the great classical poems of Homer. As even the least inspired of his later poems proved, his mastery over language never failed him. In the lines describing Ulysses' recovery from the storm in Book 5, Bryant, recapturing some of the rhythm and imagery of "Thanatopsis," gave voice to a proper epigraph for his own creative life:

> So did Ulysses, in that pile of leaves,
> Bury himself, while Pallas o'er his eyes
> Poured sleep and closed his lids, that he might take,
> After his painful toils, the fitting rest.[26]

Chapter Two

The Poems of Nature

In one of the few passages in his poetry that explicitly personifies Nature, Bryant was to express his major insight into the meaning the natural world had for him:

> To him who in the love of Nature holds
> Communion with her visible forms, she speaks
> A various language . . .

Though these lines are, of course, a prelude to a consideration of the theme of death, they could well serve as an introduction to Bryant's work as a whole. For the end product of his "communion" was not—as it was for many of his contemporaries—a pure delight, or solace, or simplification of life; it was rather a "language"—a means of expressing those values and those moods for which no other means of expression was available. Just as he learned many foreign languages during his life, Bryant was to learn readily and sensitively the language of Nature. Like Wordsworth, he endeavored to look steadily at his subject; and, like Emerson, he sought for poetic material in the least of Nature's creatures as well as in the greatest. That duality of vision—by which his inward world became fused with the birds, flowers, trees, and mountains—Bryant developed early in his career and applied to the interpretation of the "visible forms" to which his lines refer. In his most successful creations, the act of communion became a dialogue in which nature, although seldom personified, absorbed the poet's ideas and returned them to him, transformed and heightened.

This dialogue with nature, it is true, had its deadly moments as well as its creative ones. In a poem like "Innocent Child and Snow White Flower" Bryant was capable of an easy, sentimental correlation between human values and natural objects that does justice to neither. For the most part, however, the correlations and analogies are not so facile; the poems gather intensity through the resistance of nature to the glib moralizing of man. Though by temperament

Bryant was not drawn to complicated and obscure matters, nature had a way of thrusting upon him manifestly unsolvable problems. The best poems grew out of no relaxed application of obvious sentiments to appropriate landscapes but out of a dynamic process in which the poet doubted as much as he accepted, resisted as much as he asserted, and denied as much as he bestowed. The "various language" that nature spoke for Bryant was not always clear, nor was he consistently receptive; but it was the chief agency by which he was led into his poems—and into personal discoveries of meaning and value.

More specifically, there are four general areas into which Bryant's dialogue repeatedly ventured. (Two other major problems are treated in chapters 3 and 4.) First, and most important for those who would distinguish between Bryant and the British romantics, is his strong preference for the nature to be found in the United States. Second, there is Bryant's consistent identification of beauty with the fragile transience of flowers. Third, there is the habitual association of romance with a natural or pastoral setting; indeed, there is an inability to conceive of it poetically in any other context. Fourth, there is his inclination to think of personal religion almost exclusively as a communion of man with God in nature. Each of these generalizations is not a simple matter of attitude or opinion. In each of these areas the poet faced contradictions and paradoxes that are reflected in the poems themselves; and only through an examination of specific poems does Bryant's creative involvement with each of these issues become clear.

American Landscapes

In considering, first, the preference of the poet for American native scenery, it is most useful to compare two poems in blank verse: one, a response to an American landscape; the other, a response to a foreign scene. The first, Bryant's widely anthologized poem "The Prairies" (1833) is perhaps his most enthusiastic paean to the New World. Only Whitman was to rival his vivid sense of American open spaces and to make it symbolic of the spread-eagle nationalism of the mid–nineteenth century. Yet even in this poem nature must have its say. The triumphant spirit that was, in 1833, already becoming that of Manifest Destiny would find its counter-spirit in the very imagery by which it was expressed. The experience of the moment—the artist's vision—served to correct the extravagances of political idealism. The poem is more than a piece of patriotic, breast-beating oratory; it recognizes values more inclusive and more profound than those of political slogans.

"The Prairies" was inspired, as Bryant's notes suggest, by his first exposure to the interminable stretches of land and sky to be found in the Great Plains. He had come upon them as he traveled westward to visit his brother, a settler in southern Illinois, and his reaction was immediate and intense.[1] The overpowering impression made upon him at this time is communicated by the sweeping rhythms of the blank verse and by the sharp, plentiful imagery of the poem. Indeed, the pressures of spontaneous emotion upon the poet, as he set about composing this lyric, were great enough to make him forego his customary introduction and to dive into the substance of the poem with an emphatic "These . . .":

> These are the gardens of the Desert, these
> The unshorn fields, boundless and beautiful,
> For which the speech of England has no name—
> The Prairies. I behold them for the first,
> And my heart swells, while the dilated sight
> Takes in the encircling vastness.

From such paeans as this, of course, continental empires are made. The breezes that pass warmly across this plain

>   have played
> Among the palms of Mexico and vines
> Of Texas, and have crisped the limpid brooks
> That from the fountains of Sonora glide
> Into the calm Pacific . . .

The nationalistic strain develops in lines of praise to distinctly American characteristics beyond those of topography: flora (high rank grass), fauna (bison), and archaeological evidences (those curious formations left by the mound builders). These mounds are, however, reminders of the insignificance of man's works in the universal scale; and the mood of the poet momentarily contends with the patriot's enthusiasm:

> Man hath no part in all this glorious work:
> The hand that built the firmament hath heaved

> And smoothed these verdant swells, and
>   sown their slopes
> With herbage, planted them with island-groves,
> And hedged them round with forests.

Thereupon, these lines on the past gradually immerse the poet in less sanguine reflections on human progress:

> Thus change the forms of being. Thus arise
> Races of living things, glorious in strength,
> And perish, as the quickening breath of God
> Fills them, or is withdrawn.

Even this is not conclusive, however, and the flux of the poem— between the immediate majesty of the scene and the associations it evokes in the mind of the historically conscious poet—continues. The overwhelming beauty, abundance, and vitality of the scene before him draw the poet out of the past into the immediate experience of the present:

> Still this great solitude is quick with life.
> Myriads of insects, gaudy as the flowers
> They flutter over, gentle quadrupeds,
> And birds, that scarce have learned
>   the fear of man,
> Are here, and sliding reptiles of the ground,
> Startlingly beautiful.

Such delight, continues this dialogue of the poet with nature, can only promise a rich future. The pervasive sound of the bees, a "domestic hum," is converted by the imagination into the other noises of eventual settlement:

> The sound of that advancing multitude
> Which soon shall fill these deserts.
>   From the ground
> Comes up the laugh of children, the soft voice
> Of maidens, and the sweet and solemn hymn
> Of Sabbath worshippers.

Again the historical consciousness wanes, the vision of prosperous nationalism fades into the perception of the moment, and Nature speaks once more her "various language": "All at once / A fresher wind sweeps by, and breaks my dream, / And I am in the wilderness alone."[2]

With this radical reversal in mood, the poem closes, leaving the reader suspended between the alternative ideas and emotions that the poet has extracted from his experience. "The Prairies" is, thus, illustrative of Bryant's treatment of nature in his better poems, particularly those in blank verse; but it differs from them in one important respect. It is one of the few poems that takes place in the open solitude rather than in the intimate glade or brookside retreat. Nor is the perspective of the poem that of the fashionable "picturesque" with those neat, rectangularly framed vistas that the eighteenth century had enjoyed. Rather the vision, which Bryant describes as that of "dilated sight," is a vision of plenitude as it pours in upon the sensibility from all sides, a fullness of experience in the face of which the poet can only record the ebb and flow of his emotional life.

All in all, "The Prairies" is a very convincing and compelling work, not because it is the springing to life of a hypothesis—the greatness and promise of America—in an appropriately spontaneous fashion, but because it is a complete realization by the poetic intelligence of what it means to entertain this hypothesis. Bryant was not, as Whitman was to be, temperamentally or intellectually ready to take the optimistic plunge into the benevolent cosmos. His dream must break, leaving him "in the wilderness alone." But this is the source of the poem's strength, even though it may be a source of philosophical confusion. If the sublime aesthetics of the national spirit were one order of truth that the poet could express through the medium of natural imagery, there was another order of truth that placed man, as an autonomous consciousness, apart and isolated from the natural phenomena he perceived. "The Prairies" does not reconcile these truths, but it forcefully expresses the dilemma of the romantic sensibility as it sought political conviction in a dream of America the Beautiful.

"Earth," composed two years later, in 1834, approached the problem of national sentiment in an entirely different manner. The sensibility of the poet encountered not a vast stage for heroic enterprise in nature but a formless and ominous night. The historical consciousness, instead of providing a release from the immediate scene, tended to intensify a melancholy experience. The imagery, instead of conveying a vivid sense of natural detail, was blurred and dusky. As the first strophe suggests, "Earth" is closer to Matthew Arnold's "Dover Beach" than it is to Whitman's "Passage to India":

> A midnight black with clouds is in the sky;
> I seem to feel, upon my limbs, the weight
> Of its vast brooding shadow. All in vain
> Turns the tired eye in search of form; no star
> Pierces the pitchy veil; no ruddy blaze,
> From dwellings lighted by the cheerful hearth,
> Tinges the flowering summits of the grass.
> No sound of life is heard, no village hum.
> Nor measured tramp of footstep in the path,
> Nor rush of wind, while, on the breast of Earth,
> I lie and listen to her mighty voice:
> A voice of many tones—sent up from streams
> That wander through the gloom, from woods unseen
> Swayed by the sweeping of the tides of air,
> From rocky chasms where darkness dwells all day,
> And hollows of the great invisible hills,
> And sands that edge the ocean, stretching far
> Into the night—a melancholy sound!

Why the eye is "tired" and why the "mighty voice" of Earth is melancholy seem to be explained by the memory of past wars, injustices, bloodshed, and terror. Even the "glens and groves" now "murmur of guilty force and treachery." The poet's consciousness of the past merges with his memories of personal grief. He attempts to identify his sorrow with that of Earth and thus find expression for his own depression in Nature's language: "O Earth! dost thou too sorrow for the past / Like man thy offspring? Do I hear thee mourn / Thy childhood's unreturning hours . . .?"

Yet this process of identification is too costly, for it plunges the poet from one level of despair deeper into murky areas from which he is hard put to recover. At one point the language verges upon the erotic, as the images of Earth and dead loved ones are momentarily synthesized: "Alone, in darkness, on thy naked soil, / The mighty nourisher and burial-place / Of man, I feel that I embrace their dust."

In the lines immediately following, however, this implicit longing for death is replaced by a deeper murmur at which the poet

begins to "tremble at its dreadful import." Nature throws back
upon him not merely the evil of the historical past but also what
seem to be references to personal guilt: "The dust of her who loved
and was betrayed, / And him who died neglected in his age . . ."[3]
Line after line the images of wronged humanity accumulate to provide a Gothic gallery for which there would seem to be no atonement,
no resolution, no compensating mood.

Yet the ready answer had been spelled out in "The Prairies" and
in numbers of other poems. Nature in the Old World was soiled
by civilization; nature in the New World gave promise of bright
things to come. The concluding strophes of "Earth" seek an equilibrium for the poem in this comforting idea. Thus, the key to the
poem, delayed until this crucial moment, is now provided:

> Here, where I rest, the vales of Italy
> Are round me, populous from early time,
> And field of the tremendous warfare waged
> 'Twixt good and evil. Who, alas! shall dare
> Interpret to man's ear the mingled voice
> That comes from her old dungeons . . .

Earth has not, after all, spoken—only the "mingled voice" of those
historical excrescences to be found in "the vales of Italy." Yet even
if this murmur with which the poet has conducted his dialogue is
not that of nature in its pristine purity, the issue has been raised:
Is there hope that mankind can ever outrun its history and return
to the state of moral innocence—even in the brave New World?

Bryant attempts, not altogether successfully, to answer this question with a qualified "yes." The mood of the poem as a whole is
not easily ignored, and his affirmation is reduced to a rather pallid
rhetorical question:

> O thou,
> Who sittest far beyond the Atlantic deep,
> Among the sources of thy glorious streams,
> My native Land of Groves! a newer page
> In the great record of the world is thine;
> Shall it be fairer? Fear, and friendly Hope,
> And Envy, watch the issue, while the lines,
> By which thou shalt be judged, are written down.[4]

Together, "The Prairies" and "Earth" illustrate the potential strengths and weaknesses of Bryant's efforts to test his patriotic assumptions in a creative experiment. Although these poems are quite different in many ways, they both encounter a language of discovery, and, in consequence, each acquires a complexity and distinctiveness quite unusual in patriotic hymns.

The Transient Flowers

Simple emotions were not Bryant's forte. The almost prosaic language of his verses and the general clarity of the dramatic situations of the poems are too often deceptive. Even his little verses on flowers, as unpretentious and subdued as they appear, are not pure expressions of delight and admiration. Inhibiting the emotional impulse that brings the poet to the exquisite and delicate subject matter of violets, gentians, and windflowers is not only the artist's sense of form but also an intelligence alert to physical and moral relationships. Instead of simplicity, these poems contain an involvement and intricacy that is their real merit. Furthermore, what they may lose in lyrical power is often compensated for by the poet's insight into the fullness of his experience.

That these poems can be read—and too often are—as polite sketches with appended moral sentiments is unfortunate; yet such misinterpretations reflect Bryant's own dilemma in the face of natural beauty. Does nature, after all, unite beauty and moral truth within the same discernible objects, or are there two quite distinct orders of value? At times Bryant writes as though beauty necessarily entails some sort of certitude and has its own authority; but the more successful poems, three of which shall be briefly treated here, imply that it is the imagination of the poet and the human capacity to formulate experiences into art that ultimately unifies value with perception, truth with beauty.

Best known of these three is "The Yellow Violet," composed when Bryant was twenty years of age. Central to this quiet lyric is the idea that this blossom appears in April as a harbinger of spring. The opening stanza accurately pinpoints the time of year and briefly captures the visual image of the flower as it is found in its natural habitat:

> When beechen buds begin to swell,
> And woods the blue-bird's warble know,

The yellow violet's modest bell
Peeps from the last year's leaves below.

The second stanza introduces the speaker in the poem and imposes upon the scene his rather vague emotion: "Sweet flower, I love, in forest bare, / To meet thee. . . ." From this point through the remaining six stanzas, the poem is—as Professor George Arms has suggested—essentially dramatic.[5] The flower and narrator are participants in a dialogue that rises to a disclosure and eventual climax. Neither the intrinsic beauty of the flower nor the poet's delight upon discovering it lie at the heart of the verses, but instead the subject is an awareness, which is all but mutual, of the degree of human pride involved in any observation of natural forms:

Oft, in the sunless April day,
Thy early smile has stayed my walk;
But midst the gorgeous blooms of May,
I passed thee on thy humble stalk.

So they, who climb to wealth, forget
The friends in darker fortunes tried.
I copied them—but I regret
That I should ape the ways of pride.[6]

Simply to pass this off as "moralism" is to miss the unfolding of the poem and its play of delight against reflection. Does the violet remind the poet of guilt incurred in his social relations, or does the metaphor of the social climber serve to explain man's neglect of the humble beauties of nature? To reread these lines with this question in mind is to grasp the complexity of Bryant's aesthetic. My answer is that the poem has it both ways and that this is the essence of the dramatic dialogue. Thus, the concluding stanza can be read, both literally and figuratively, as a statement about man's moral relationship to nature *and* as a comment upon one's social obligations:

And when again the genial hour
Awakes the painted tribes of light,
I'll not o'erlook the modest flower
That made the woods of April bright.

Complementary to "The Yellow Violet," to the extent that it deals with the last lingering blossom of autumn instead of the first to appear in spring, is "To the Fringed Gentian." There are no feelings of regret aroused by this flower; in fact, four of the five stanzas sing clearly and sweetly of its blue brightness and of the cold, bare setting in which it appears. Although the plant is apostrophized, there is no intrusion of the first-person pronoun and no imposition of the speaker's feelings upon the subject matter—until the final stanza. There the rational element, staved off for sixteen lines, must have its say. Moved by the barrenness of the passing year to consider his own demise and "the hour of death," the poet sees in the flower an emblem of "Hope, blossoming within my heart." The full text of "To the Fringed Gentian" is as follows:

> Thou blossom bright with autumn dew
> And colored with the heaven's own blue,
> That openest when the quiet light
> Succeeds the keen and frosty night—
>
> Thou comest not when violets lean
> O'er wandering brooks and springs unseen,
> Or columbines, in purple dressed,
> Nod o'er the ground-bird's hidden nest.
>
> Thou waitest late and com'st alone,
> When woods are bare and birds are flown,
> And frosts and shortening days portend
> The aged year is near his end.
>
> Then doth thy sweet and quiet eye
> Look through its fringes to the sky,
> Blue—blue—as if that sky let fall
> A flower from its cerulean wall.
>
> I would that thus, when I shall see
> The hour of death draw near to me,
> Hope, blossoming within my heart,
> May look to heaven as I depart.[7]

The metaphor that equates Hope with the blue flower crystallizes an entire train of reflection that has run submerged through the poem. The concern of the narrator for the desolation of approaching winter, his feeling for the solitary nature of the flower, and his

association of the flower's blue with that of the heavens have all
been steps toward the realization expressed in the final lines. The
statement of moral meaning may be overly explicit, but it is by no
means gratuitous: it comes as the fruit of the observation and reflection of a human being strongly infected with the quality of a
late autumn walk. Not only do these lines extract human meaning
from a chance contact with the fringed gentian, but also they cast
back upon nature itself a solemn appreciation of its dignified movement through the cycle of life and death. For the poet, in his
restrained appeal that he, too, might die as Nature dies (with hope
for regeneration), has added a further dimension to the experience.
The small flower and its local setting are perceived within some
greater context—call it time—in which both men and natural objects move. This appeal of the poet is, thus, a delayed recognition
of the empathetic relationship between man and flower.

In the third of these flower poems, "The Death of the Flowers,"
Bryant has used a similar structural device. Instead of delaying his
articulation of the theme of the poem, however, he withholds the
key to the dramatic situation. By skillful treatment of the autumnal
passing of the summer flowers, he creates a fine balance between
pathos and detachment. The eventual, inevitable passage of beautiful
things is established as the theme of the poem; and the full sense
of what is meant by the opening line, "The melancholy days have
come, the saddest of the year," is developed in every line. The third
stanza, for example, sustains the mood while offering only the slight-
est hint ("the plague on men") as to the basic situation:

The wind-flower and the violet, they perished long ago,
And the brier rose and the orchis died amid the summer glow,
But on the hill the golden-rod, and the aster in the wood,
And the yellow sunflower by the brook in autumn beauty stood,
Till fell the frost from the clear cold heaven, as falls the plague on men,
And the brightness of their smile was gone, from upland, glade, and glen.[8]

Thus, the disclosure in the fifth stanza that the proper object of
the lament is not the flowers—that they have only served as symbolic
substitutes for the young girl who has died—does not come as a
shock but as an honest recognition of the inexorable bond between
beauty and death. The imagery of the flowers, the mood of early
winter, and the rhythms set in motion by the descriptive verses

give to this concluding stanza of "The Death of the Flowers" a restrained tension that is a marvelous achievement. The effect is that of the slow rising to conscious articulation of buried, inexpressible grief and of the vast sense of relief that comes from the poet's ability to objectify the experience:

And then I think of one who in her youthful beauty died,
The fair meek blossom that grew up and faded by my side.
In the cold moist earth we laid her, when the forests cast the leaf,
And we wept that one so lovely should have a life so brief:
Yet not unmeet it was that one, like that young friend of ours,
So gentle and so beautiful, should perish with the flowers.

Romance in Nature

The use of natural imagery in this poem as a means for describing the feeling attendant upon the death of a beautiful young girl introduces one of the most muddled and baffling aspects of romantic poetry. The beautiful girl, so runs one line of thought, is nature's innocent child—Wordsworth's Lucy—whose loveliness derives from qualities quite apart from her sexuality. Yet she dies. Is it the awareness of the gross complexity of the world that kills her? A disdain for her animal nature? Or is it simply the order of nature that beauty passes in a day and is gone? The entire subject is shrouded in conflicting ideas and emotions, but the poet finds in this very ambiguity the material that his imagination requires. Here is a more profoundly ethical poetry than that of the land or that of floral beauty. Out of his own divided feelings about natural man (Is there a "natural woman" also?), about chastity (Is it of God and Nature?), and about the relative merits of love and passion (Can the higher be reached without the lower?) Bryant fashioned his lyrics of maidens in nature.

What should be observed, however, is the persistence of a male perspective. As feminist criticism has brought to our attention, the imposition of male perspectives and male concerns upon women shaped and shaded much of the fiction and poetry of the nineteenth century.[9] It is not that imaginative writers such as Bryant were insensitive to the particular modes of feminine thought and feeling, but rather that they were too often limited by their poetics, their vocabulary, and the mores of the age from articulating them. Thus, the "Death of the Flowers" is about male grief—the man's appreciation of her gentleness and physical beauty—rather than whatever the young woman herself may have felt about her demise. When Bryant writes of his women in nature, it is either from a position, unintentional but obvious enough, of the somewhat superior male, or, as will be shortly demonstrated, by resorting to the subterfuge of depicting women outside of the middle-class mainstream of American life.

Take, for example, the widely anthologized "Oh Fairest of the Rural Maids" (1820), a polite and unambitious piece of flattery directed toward Frances Fairchild, subsequently to become his wife. In the convention of Renaissance love lyrics, the name of the adored is immortalized within the poem, albeit here coyly divided and placed in the first and fifth lines (italicized):

> Oh *fair*est of the rural maids!
> Thy birth was in the forest shades;
> Green boughs, and glimpses of the sky,
> Were all that met thine infant eye.
>
> Thy sports, thy wanderings, when a *child,*
> Were ever in the sylvan wild;
> And all the beauty of the place
> Is in thy heart and on thy face. [10]

The association of the "sylvan wild" with feminine beauty passes unquestioned in the poem. No instance of nature more unrestrained than the playful wind or the silent spring arises to shatter the pretty comparison. For all the avowed compliments, however, the posture of the poet has a suggestion of condescension in it. For all the decorative imagery, the vision of his loved one is that of a child– woman without mature passion or soul. Her purity and innocence, like the virgin forest, have charm but lack substance and purpose. As the concluding stanza unintentionally makes explicit, the young woman and the woodland setting are virtuous by default:

> The forest depths, by foot unpressed,
> Are not more sinless than thy breast;
> The holy peace, that fills the air
> Of those calm solitudes, is there.

Thus, through bland assertion, the compatibility of natural beauty and moral purity are upheld, although there is equivocation in the

awkward expression, "Are not more sinless," and a straining for the
metaphor in the comparison of the undefiled female breast with
"The forest depths, by foot unpressed."

In other poems Bryant draws back from this naive commitment
to the absolute innocence of females and tends to minimize the
imposition of his male outlook. He attributes to women the capacities for passion and self-awareness. In "An Indian Maid's Lament" the young woman sings a "sad and simple lay" for her fallen
lover. "Rizpah" (1824), based upon the Old Testament story in
2 Samuel, is the frenzied cry of Rizpah's grief for her children
slaughtered by the Gibeonites:

> I have wept till I could not weep, and the pain
> Of the burning eyeballs went to my brain.
> Seven blackened corpses before me lie,
> In the blaze of the sun and the winds of the sky.[11]

The "Song of the Greek Amazon" (1824) is another resonant and
defiant lyric as voiced by a young woman whose lover was slain by
the enemy Turks. Of a more tranquil temper is "A Song of Pitcairn's
Island" (1825), in which the young Polynesian wife of one of the
British mutineer–settlers, and mother of their blue-eyed child, gives
expression to her happiness. That these are all exotics, beyond the
pale of white America, is a literary strategy that defers to the sensibility of his era.

This having been said, however, it is only fair to note that Bryant
did write a rather puzzling poem, "The Maiden's Sorrow" (1842),
which tells of a young woman, presumably homegrown, who still
after seven years grieves for her man who has died in "the distant
West." This is presented with no suggestion that seven years of
mourning is unseemly, abnormal, or pathological. And there is no
question that the grief is still intense:

> In the dreams of my lonely bed,
>   Ever thy form before me seems,
> All night long I talk with the dead,
>   All day long I think of my dreams.
>
> This deep wound that bleeds and aches,
>   This long pain, a sleepless pain—

> When the Father my spirit takes,
> I shall feel it no more again. [12]

These two concluding stanzas of despair and anguish, quite distinct
from the preceding sentimentality, anticipate "The Hill Wife" and
other of Robert Frost's darker poems. They are, however, anomalous
in Bryant's works.

Indian maidens, however, children of nature, could give vent to
their natural passions, as could no seemly blue-eyed "rural maids."
The long narrative poem "Monument Mountain" (1824) treats nature, sexuality, and passion in a mature yet sensitive way. Although
there are imitative elements in it, the poem is remarkably vivid in
its setting, consistent in its synthesis of the human and natural
elements, and of an almost classical deliberateness in its movement
to a fatal close. The tale, which gives the poem its structure, is
simply that of an Indian maiden, "bright-eyed/with a wealth of
maiden tresses":

> She loved her cousin; such a love was deemed,
> By the morality of those stern tribes,
> Incestuous, and she struggled hard and long
> Against her love, and reasoned with her heart,
> As simple Indian maiden might. [13]

After prolonged suffering she confides her troubles to a friend,
saying: " 'Thou knows'st, and thou alone,'/ . . . 'for I have told
thee all my love,/And guilt and sorrow.' " Her confession made,
she puts on the ornaments, given to her by her father, climbs with
her friend to the precipice on the mountain that commands "the
region of her tribe," and, at sunset, throws herself from the rock.

It is a tale with Hawthorne's darkness about it, and, like Melville's
novel, *Pierre,* which it may well have inspired, "Monument Mountain" treats the subject of incest in such a way that innocence itself
is made the source of grief and guilt. Also, like the major works
of Hawthorne and Melville, this poem is unified by a dominant
central symbol: the mountain that derives its name from the monument of rough stones placed there by the mourning tribes. The
mountain symbolizes Nature, not only, as we might expect, in its
permanence and immensity, but also in those qualities of beauty
and savagery as they are paradoxically combined in natural objects:

"Thou who wouldst see the the lovely and the wild / Mingled in harmony on Nature's face, / Ascend our rocky mountains."

And what is true of nature is also by implication true of natural man. Though the climber of the mountain may achieve an "expanding heart," "a kindred with a loftier world," and "The enlargement of . . . vision," the experience is not one of tranquility but an imposing mixture of peace and terror, loveliness and wildness. Even while the eye takes in "white villages, and tilth and herd," it also sees "bare old cliffs," seared by the elements to "chalky whiteness":

> . . . It is a fearful thing
> To stand upon the beetling verge, and see
> Where storm and lightning, from that huge gray wall,
> Have tumbled down vast blocks, and at the base
> Dashed them in fragments, and to lay thine ear
> Over the dizzy depth, and hear the sound
> Of winds, that struggle with the woods below,
> Come up like ocean murmurs.

The sensibility, nourished by these contradictory aspects of the scene before it, turns to the tale—the "sad tradition of unhappy love"—to find a relevance to human experience.

The poem develops dramatically from this point, tracing the impact of the outlawed desires of the maiden upon her body and her spirit. She who once was "The fairest of the Indian maids, bright-eyed, / With wealth of raven tresses, a light form, / And a gay heart," loses her gaiety, weeps in solitude, and wastes away until the sage dames of the tribe say, *"The girl will die."* To her closest friend she pours out her heart:

> . . . I am sick of life.
> All night I weep in darkness, and the morn
> Glares on me, as upon a thing accursed,
> That has no business on the earth.

The natural passion of the innocent has, as she herself recognizes, become unnatural. Only through death can she return to a state of harmony with Nature. Only death restores the balance between her beauty and her wildness.

Her suicide has its own solemn ritual: the ascent of the mountain, the wearing of ornaments associated with childhood and happier days, the day-long vigil on the mountaintop overlooking "the region of her tribe," and, particularly "the cabin-roof / Of him she loved." Indeed, this is a religious rite, for the location of her vigil, the precipice, is strewn with offerings to the tribal gods. The Indians believed "that God / Doth walk on high places," and so they share, in a more direct and primitive fashion, the feelings of exaltation of the civilized climber with his "expanded heart" and enlarged vision.

Much later in his career, Bryant reworked the theme of lost innocence into a fantasy, "Sella" (1862). This tale in blank verse tells of a young maiden, Sella, who discovers a pair of magic slippers in which she may descend beneath the surface of the stream near her family home. There, throughout her young years, she explores the wonders and beauties of submarine life, and, under the guidance of a nameless, exotic fairy, she travels downstream into the great ocean. Her parents, when they hear from her of these excursions, decide that she is a dreamer, but her brother, motivated by fear and envy of "that cold world of waters and the strange / Beings that dwell within it," eventually steals the slippers and throws them into the stream—forever out of reach. Sella accuses her family harshly, in a tone that suggests the Indian maiden's lament:

> . . . Cruel ones!
> 'Tis you who shut me out eternally
> From the serener world which I had learned
> To love so well. Why took ye not my life?[14]

This thinly veiled story of sexual awakening, also hinting of an incestuous relationship, comes, however, to a happier conclusion than "Monument Mountain." Sella finds a less catastrophic penance in acts of mercy, and she gains new strength through prayer. Her innocent adventures bear strange fruit, for she becomes a philosopher—queen, instructing her people in the mysteries of hydromechanics and teaching them to build venetian wells, viaducts, and water wheels. Throughout her life, however, she remains celibate, and, upon her death, she is buried near the stream of her childhood, under a marble monument inscribed with her name. The stream subsequently divides to flow over the grave.

The contrast between "Monument Mountain" and "Sella" does

not reflect any substantial shift in Bryant's treatment of sexuality. In both poems the metaphor of ascent (the Indian maiden climbs the mountain, while Sella emerges from the fantasy world of the sea) indicates the capacity of human beings to transcend their limitations, either self-imposed, as in Sella's case, or instilled in the conscience through tribal mores. Both poems emphasize the moral and emotional conflicts within the individual rather than any romantic or sexual contact between the girl and her lover. Indeed, the implication of these two poems is that sexuality is almost entirely an intimate, personal problem in which the loved one or society at large has little stake. Chastity is not glorified as a social ideal but as a personal standard gleaned from some contact by the uncorrupted innocent with the spiritual laws governing the universe. What distinguishes the two poems and explains the different endings is a change in Bryant's attitude toward guilt and retribution. Whereas the Indian maiden could expiate her sinful passion only through the ultimate gesture expressive of her faith, Sella was to be cleansed through a doctrine of works. But theological conceptions were foreign to Bryant, and, aside from the apparent influence of the Civil War upon his life and art, it is difficult to assess this shift in his attitude.

Piety in Nature = Devotion and Reverence

In a sense, all of Bryant's poems of nature are traceable to a concern for religious values. That this should emerge more explicitly in these two poems, where the dominant theme is the role of sexual emotion in nature and society, than it had in the poems dealing with national vistas or flowers, suggests that the deeper the poet mined his heart, the closer he came to the religious ore. The religious problem, however, even as it crops up in nature poetry, is not an isolated one. Though its balance and texture are derived from the personal experiences of the poet, these experiences take place within the larger context of his immediate society. Thus his personal religious feelings and ideas—particularly as they are expressed in "A Forest Hymn," "Inscription for the Entrance to a Wood," and "A Summer Ramble,"—bear the imprint of the intellectual revolution that had taken place in late eighteenth- and early nineteenth-century New England.

As historians have made abundantly clear, the breakdown of the

monolithic intellectual system of Calvinism in New England and
the passing flurry of enlightened Deism in the late eighteenth century had left large vacuums in the religious lives of the Protestant
middle class with which Bryant identified himself. In particular,
there was lacking the vital center of emotional conviction, without
which neither the remnant disciples of the old Puritanism nor the
liberals, chief among whom were the Unitarians, could hope to
survive. Although the function of revivalism in prolonging the life
of the Calvinist genus is not our proper concern here, it was one
means by which emotionalism, "enthusiasm" in the theological
terminology of the day, could be respectably reinstated into community life. It provided a convenient bridge, as Wordsworthian
lyricism was also to do, between the narrow sphere of private piety
and the communal ground of institutionalized society.

The liberal churches did not, quite naturally, turn from Bible
and sacraments to the pursuit of the God of Nature, and thus too
rigorous a parallelism between pietistic revivalism and lyric poetry
can only obscure our point. What was held in common was a motive
rather than a practice: a sense that American individualism meant
more than an atomistic relationship between members of the body
politic—it meant that the individual could become emotionally and
intellectually, for certain heightened moments at least, the recep-
tacle of the living universe. The great metaphors of revivalism—
Jesus the Redeemer, Salvation, Heaven—penetrated to the core of
personal life as the doctrines of the Atonement, Predestination, and
Election had, by 1800, ceased to do for the mass of men. Conversely,
the liberal consciousness, its initial awe of a Newtonian machine-
universe rubbed thin, turned to an image of the Creator with which
the heart might make contact, a beneficent Father whose construction of the natural order, according to the revealed laws of physics,
was accompanied by generous goodwill toward men. William Ellery
Channing set the tone for nineteenth-century Unitarianism, but
such hymns as "The Earth is Full of Thy Riches," written by Bryant
while still at Great Barrington in 1820, lent further support to the
movement to unite science with sentiment:

> ALMIGHTY! hear thy children raise
> The voice of thankfulness and praise,
> To Him whose wisdom deigned to plan
> This fair and bright abode for man.

> For when this orb of sea and land
> Was moulded in thy forming hand,
> Thy calm, benignant smile impressed
> A beam of heaven upon its breast. [15]

Even though our analysis is too general to do justice to the complex social history of the early nineteenth century, it does shed considerable light upon the lyricism of Bryant's poetry. For, like the revivalist, Bryant had no new theology—not even a novel weltanschauung—to offer, only new life to breathe into accepted conceptions. As Whitehead and others have observed, romantic poetry about nature may have resisted the mechanism of eighteenth-century science, but the magnificent vision of a universe made orderly and whole remained undiminished. Thus, Bryant differs from an enlightened poet like Freneau not because he rejects natural philosophy, but because his lyricism travels farther down the road of personal involvement with the facts of nature. True, he stopped short of the kind of organic relationship with natural facts of which Emerson was to preach and of which Whitman was to sing; thus he remains the natural philosopher rather than the transcendentalist. His involvement, however, prompts him to break through the scientific abstractions that define the order of nature in a way that Freneau, even in "The Wild Honeysuckle," could only approximate. And in this convergence of poetry with natural fact, which also entailed the dissipation of "scientific" systems, classifications, and simple cause-and-effect relationships, a genuine and deeply felt reverence for things was born. In the face of nature on his rambles and in the brookside meditations, that rational knowledge of the poet first gave way to sensation, groped its way back toward understanding, and then unified the stream of experience within his poem.

The failure of our contemporary readers to respond to Bryant's pious nature poetry is symptomatic. Science, having long since abandoned the obvious evidences of order—such as would strike the eye of Sunday strollers or bird watchers—has left us indifferent before natural objects, save for those which overwhelm us with sensory stimuli. For the nineteenth century, however, still laboriously sifting genera and species, still pondering the enormous scale of geological ages, still deciphering the mysterious laws that govern comets, natural facts were neither too remote to be interesting nor too complex to forestall rational consideration. Thus it was that the magnificent "Creator" or "First Cause" of Newton could be glimpsed, in moments of intensity, only a few paces beyond normal vision, lurking behind woodland oaks and impelling birds in their flight. It does no real harm if modern critics and scholars thrust the label of pantheism upon his poetry; one form of heresy is, I suppose, as good as another. What must be borne in mind, nevertheless, is that Bryant's *theology* differs in no essential way from the Christian rationalism of the eighteenth century. Systematic thought brought him not closer to God, and God closer to nature, but closer to mood, reverie, and observation. This piety we cannot share had its source not in logic but in experience, and only thus can it be comprehended.

Howard Mumford Jones took this emphasis upon the experiential basis of Bryant's theology one step further. He argues that Bryant is essentially a stoic, a "premature existentialist" who was a Christian in only the broadest sense:

Bryant is the poet of elemental forces—death and life, the seasons, storm and calm, the sea, the wind, the snow, but he is not a Christian "nature" poet as Whittier or Longfellow is. Indeed, if one is to save this melancholy spirit for Christian poetry, one is almost tempted to define him as a Christian who fell into the heresy of Manichaenism—that the struggle between darkness and light, between tragedy and calm, between good and evil, is his central reading of the Christian faith. It is unorthodox to say so, but I feel, in studying Bryant, that his Christianity was a piece of personal sincerity that cannot be questioned, and that so far as his world view is concerned, Christianity is for him an outward and modern symbol of an ancient and more primitive faith. [16]

While one can grant the "elemental" quality in Bryant's poetry, and certainly accept that he differs from the other "household" poets in this respect, the allegation of Manichaen assumptions is dubious. Bryant, to the contrary, shared the liberal faith of his era that darkness and evil were unfortunate aberrations of an imperfect world, not the manifestations of demonic energies at loose in the cosmos.

Whatever conjectures we might make as to what Bryant did or did not believe, it is important to realize that he never articulated them in a systematic way. Poems such as "Inscription for the Entrance to a Wood," "A Forest Hymn," and "A Summer Ramble" were confessions rather than credos. They are, after all, neither statements of faith nor philosophical treatises; they are simply accounts of what happened to a receptive individual in the face of nature. The philosophical framework is just that—a framework—for within it mood, reflection, and speculation play in a highly unpredictable fashion.

The synthesizing process by which Bryant created these poems is most evident in "A Forest Hymn" (1825). Fundamentally a reasoned statement in verse about the appropriateness of worshipping God in natural surroundings, this poem gathers a particular drive of its own as it develops, and it soon discards argumentation as its structural device.

The rational abstractions serve their purpose, however, in providing a firm, credible foundation for the highly personal superstructure. Protestants would find familiar contrasts between the ways of simpler virtue and "human pomp or pride." They would find intellectual satisfaction in the argument that the woods are a purer place of worship than man-made edifices because "No fantastic carvings show / The boast of our vain race to change the form / Of thy fair works."[17] The mind could agree that the values of "grandeur, strength, and grace" are exemplified in the natural objects to be found within the forest. In the life-and-death cycle evidenced by the mold of decaying vegetation there is, certainly, "The lesson of thy own eternity." Though there have been "holy men" who have given themselves up to lives of "thought and prayer" in the wilderness, it suffices, says the voice of moderation, to retire "often to these solitudes." And, finally, the forest serves as a distinct reminder of the tokens of God's power—tempests, whirlwinds, and tidal waves—all of which tame man's pride and return him to a realization of God's omnipotence.

As a series of abstractions these statements are vaguely satisfying, voicing as they do the convictions of a liberalized Protestantism. But it is in the diction of this poem, rather than in its structured argument, that feeling brims with precision and intensity. Particularly in the second division of the poem, immediately following the lines on "the boast of our vain race," the poet breaks from his moralistic moorings to address a God directly perceived; the poem moves from a hymn to the First Cause to a lyric prayer to the personal deity of the poet:

> . . . But thou art here—thou fill'st
> The solitude. Thou art in the soft winds

> That run along the summit of these trees
> In music; thou art in the cooler breath
> That from the inmost darkness of the place
> Comes, scarcely felt; the barky trunks, the ground,
> The fresh moist ground, are all instinct with thee.

It is with the "barky trees" that observation sharpens, and, in the phrases reflecting the process of contemplation itself—"the ground, / The fresh moist ground"—the accumulation of natural fact begins. In rapid succession follow a bird, herbs, the spring, an oak, each absorbed into the generalization regarding God's presence, but also re-creating the experience of private communion with nature. The last lines of this division press to the ultimate the poet's apprehension of the spiritual reality of the occurrence within the forest scene:

> That delicate forest flower,
> With scented breath and look so like a smile,
> Seems, as it issues from the shapeless mould,
> An emanation of the indwelling Life,
> A visible token of the upholding Love,
> That are the soul of this great universe.

This is the core of piety in a poem that might otherwise have been merely conventionally religious. This is the momentary baring of the vital center of the religious life. That the doctrine of immanence runs counter to the poet's rational convictions regarding the order of the universe and the status of natural objects as "tokens" of the Creator's power and goodness signifies the imaginative vitality of the poem. Within the context of "The Forest Hymn" this momentary perception makes perfectly good sense, for of what use is the return to nature's temple if God is not there? Emerson and Whitman, once the way had been made clear, could raise to the level of reflective affirmation the idea that "love works at the centre" ("The Sphinx") and "the kelson of the creation is Love" ("Song of Myself"). For Bryant, the discovery was the fruit of the imaginative process, not its premise, and it had to be won anew with each successive lyric.

When read with this principle of discovery in mind, "Inscription for the Entrance to a Wood" and "A Summer Ramble" lose some of the staleness that nineteenth-century poetry has for many readers.

"Inscription begins with a plea for the "Stranger," tired of the "guilt and misery" of the world, to "enter this wild wood / And view the haunts of Nature." It briefly develops the proposition that "God hath yoked to guilt / Her pale tormentor, misery," and it draws the questionable conclusion (invalid, if restated as a syllogism) that, being without guilt, "these shades / Are still the abodes of gladness." With this expression, however, the liberal theology fades and sensory delights pour in upon poet and reader until reflection is almost totally in abeyance, leaving the quality of the experience itself to reign unchallenged.[18]

Similarly in "A Summer Ramble," once the formal recognition is made that "the plants and breathing things [are] The sinless, peaceful works of God," there is no longer reference to the Deity by name, realist overwhelms nominalist, and "the lovely landscape round" speaks for itself. It is the "deep quiet" of the tranquil scene, as the final lines declare so simply, that this "Shall be the peace whose holy smile / Welcomes him to a happier shore."[19]

Even while this lyric piety before the things of God's Nature liberated the poet from human suffering and conflict and from the confines of the ratiocinative process, it also made for limitations and restrictions. The paradoxes implicit in the representations of patriotic scenery, of beauty in nature, and of natural woman should also have indicated the fruitful perversity of the language of Nature. But there is no more blatant, or embarrassing, example of the inner contradictions created by Bryant's attempt to fuse natural religion and human values than in his poem titled "Hymn of the City."

To judge this poem by the standard of the author's intent is to deem it a failure. "Hymn of the City" is obviously intended to complement "A Forest Hymn" and to make the point that:

> Not in the solitude
> Alone may man commune with Heaven, or see,
> Only in savage wood
> And sunny vale, the present Deity . . .
>
> Even here do I behold
> Thy steps, Almighty!—here, amid the crowd
> Through the great city rolled . . .[20]

But how is God made evident in the city? Only by comparison between the details of city life and the familiar imagery of nature can the voice of the Deity be heard. The sound of the "winds whisper and the waves rejoice" finds a substitute in the noise of the crowd—the "everlasting murmur deep and loud." While the physical substance of the city is passed off as "proud piles, the work of human kind," the concluding stanzas of the poem are rich with the imagery of sun, sea, and tempest. And to confirm our suspicion that it is not really the bustle of the crowd that reveals God's spirit, the coda of the poem describes the city in its eventual return to harmonious solitude, "vast and helpless" while it sleeps.

In a later, more honest appraisal of the city, "The Crowded Street," Bryant weighed the balance heavily against urban life and emphasized the pervasive sense of futility and indifference of the city dwellers. For neither the orderly values of scientific rationalism nor the aesthetic pieties of nature worship were applicable to the new industrial civilization. Not until Whitman's "Crossing Brooklyn Ferry" was a poem to appear that could successfully incorporate urban images and rhythms in a meaningful synthesis.

If nature poetry was to draw much of its power from religious experience, however, it faced the great dilemma well known to the saints and mystics of the West. Subsequent to the tidal flow of illumination must come the slow ebbing of grace. What has been lived can only be remembered, not relived; the poet, like the saint, must seek his inspiration in time as best he can. Bryant revealed, in passages, a partial recognition of such a waning sensitivity. Both "The Old Man's Counsel" and "Among the Trees" have rather fine lines recognizing the pathos of this loss. In the former, the old man compares the perceptual life to the rising crescendo and gradual diminution of the love-signal of the partridge. Life in its later stages, like a boat on the rapid, "Darts by so swiftly that their images / Dwell not upon the mind, or only dwell / In dim confusion. . . ."[21]

"Among the Trees" (1868), however, is the attempt of the aging poet to recapture his lost sensibility. It opens in the familiar setting of trees and springs, and it apostrophizes the trees in the conventional manner. Instead of building toward a moment of lyric realization, the poet conducts an unanswered monologue:

> Have ye no sense of being? Does the air,
> The pure air, which I breathe with gladness, pass
> In gushes o'er your delicate lungs, your leaves,

> All unenjoyed? When on your winter's sleep
> The sun shines warm, have ye no dreams of spring?[22]

And so on for another twenty-one lines—the plight of articulate man in the face of his dumb environment. Lacking his answer, the poet resorts to half-hearted affirmation, but the lyric compulsion has passed him by:

> Nay, doubt we not that under the rough rind,
> In the green veins of these fair growths of earth,
> There dwells a nature that receives delight
> From all the gentle processes of life,
> And shrinks from loss of being. Dim and faint
> May be the sense of pleasure and of pain,
> As in our dreams; but, haply, real still.

The remainder of the poem develops, with some success, two leading ideas: first, the lack of sympathy that nature holds for man ("Our sorrows touch you not"); and second, the superior survival power of natural objects ("Ye have no history"). These melancholy themes, even though lacking in complete integration into this poem, look forward to the material of twentieth-century poetry.

As difficult as it is to find convincing passages of true lyricism in his later poetry, the God of nature Bryant had worshiped in his youth did not disappear with the years. Thus it is that, drawing from the writings of Boethius, he could write in the 1860s (in the decade following the publication of *The Origin of Species*) these triumphant lines from "The Order of Nature":

> While the Great Founder, he who gave these laws,
>   Holds the firm reins and sits amid his skies
> Monarch and Master, Origin and Cause,
>   And Arbiter supremely just and wise.
>
> He guides the force he gave; his hand restrains
>   And curbs it to the circle it must trace:
> Else the fair fabric which his power sustains
>   Would fall to fragments in the void of space.[23]

Theology intact, in spite of his loss of personal contact with nature, he could still speak boldly and militantly of the harmony and order of natural law.

The thesis of this discussion—that Bryant found in nature a "various language" through which he was enabled to conduct a dialogue and embark on a series of "discoveries"—has implications that extend far beyond Bryant or his poems. That it says something about romanticism, both in the United States and in Europe, that it relates to the search for a style on the part of the modern artist, that it probes at the hidden roots of transcendentalism—both as an aesthetic theory and as a religious philosophy—will be evident to the students of literature and of the history of culture. Later chapters shall be more directly concerned with several of these implications, but for the present, it will suffice to recognize the poems of nature for what they are: the products of an active, creative imagination as it explored the possibilities of expression to be found in the hypothesis that nature was language. Even a partial recognition of this element in the poems will make obsolete the notion that Bryant wrote a kind of descriptive verse to which he affixed sentiments palatable to his readers. The case is a strong one that Bryant composed the bulk of his work as a synthesis of his deepest feeling and most serious thought. In this spirit his poems deserve to be considered.

Chapter Three
The Poem of Death

The opening lines of "Thanatopsis" explicitly announce that the poet's dialogue with nature is central in this great poem. Yet the theme of death—death as it pertains immediately and personally to the poet—introduces elements that set this relationship between man and nature apart from those examined in the previous chapter. This theme, by virtue of its concern with the problem of consciousness, calls into question not only the meaning of the dialogue but the very possibility of its being conducted at all. For the dialogue was founded upon the assumption that all experience contains two absolute ingredients: a subject and an object. Bryant was never to criticize this inviolate dualism instilled in the Western mind by Descartes and Locke, and even those moments of ecstatic insight to be found in the religious poems were to respect the sharp distinction between the observer and the observed, between the poet and nature, between consciousness and material fact. But death, which destroys consciousness, ignores this distinction. Its presence—or even the threat of its presence—seems to deny the existence of a separate, autonomous sensibility capable of standing apart from its environment. The grave with its dank, dissolving remnants of humanity is the symbolic answer of that implacable monist—Nature—to all of the poet's inquiries and speculations concerning death.

Thus, to the difficulties already inherent in Bryant's creative process, the theme of death added philosophical and artistic problems of a much wider scope than he encountered in his other poems. Only in "Thanatopsis" was he able to rise above the involvements and contradictions posed by this theme. Only in "Thanatopsis" was he able to adapt the dialogue and the loose associationism of his blank verse to a structured, consistent discourse. The other poems about death, as the subsequent discussion shall point out, were fragmentary, equivocal, or, at best, evasive in their handling of this theme. Why "Thanatopsis" survived its trials while the others failed is not easy to determine, but the key to its mastery and power seems to lie in its curious career of premature publication and consistent

revision. As this chapter will explain, Bryant's progress through at
least three versions of the poem during half a decade lured him
deeper and deeper into its heart. The ultimate product, "Thanatopsis" as it emerged in the 1821 edition of his poems, was a
curiously synthetic work composed of a number of quite unstable
elements held in a state of artistic equilibrium.[1]

Contrasts with Christian Attitudes

The crux of the poem is, as many commentators have recognized,
that there are consolations for the inevitable end of human existence
quite aside from the Christian promise of eternal life. The greater
part of "Thanatopsis" is a summary catalog of these consolations,
both human and natural, that are sufficient to sustain and soothe
the individual as he approaches the grave. "Thanatopsis" is not a
refutation of the doctrine of immortality. Although it is obviously
addressed to the sensibility of those who have found scant comfort
in this doctrine, the poem completely avoids any confrontation of
religious problems, either on the theological or on emotional levels.
The problem successfully attacked in "Thanatopsis" is not what
happens to the soul in death but to the human mind.

And it is a mistake to read into the poem either our personal
religious doubts or to attribute to Bryant, in this instance, any
heretical denial of basic Christian doctrine.[2] The tendency of criticism has been to equate the shifts in Bryant's attitude toward death,
culminating in "Thanatopsis," with his espousal of liberal religion.
But the fact is that his hymns written for the Unitarian hymnal
assert at several points the doctrine of immortal life, and they thus
establish beyond question Bryant's personal belief. The hymns share
with "Thanatopsis," as we shall see presently, the deliberate omission of moralistic attitudes toward death, but otherwise are completely different in their orientation. The hymns are suppliant
addresses to God; "Thanatopsis" is a dialogue with nature.

For Bryant to divest himself completely of the Christian concepts,
even for artistic purposes, was no easy matter; for his childhood
religious background, his reading in the so-called graveyard poets,
and his respect for established modes of thought, all conspired to
lead him directly from experience into ontological problems. Indeed,
the irony of the poem is that so much from the Christian tradition

is freely borrowed to express an exclusively secular point of view. Yet out of his materials Bryant fashioned one of the few major works that speaks directly to the rationalist, empiricist mentality. "Thanatopsis" is a complex poem not because of any obscurity or ambiguity—Bryant was nothing if not lucid—but because it places a pungent new wine in old mellow bottles. Its comprehensive statement about death, still satisfactory today to many intellectuals, was somehow fashioned out of bits and pieces of biblical lore, pulpit oratory, and pious verse. The artistic success was hard-won, for both thought and sentiment tended, it seems, to follow well-worn ruts. Yet the poem's limited point of view and its carefully restricted emotional appeal remained inviolate as each successive revision defined the problem more closely and, ultimately, brought to it a satisfying resolution.

Bryant's use of his materials is further illustrated by his literary borrowing from two poems he was reading at approximately the same time he began "Thanatopsis." Both of these are staunchly orthodox in their theology. Bishop Porteus' "Death" praised, in Augustan imagery and meter, a Christ who had taught men how to die by his noble example. Robert Blair's "The Grave" evoked a long parade of ghostly horrors before dramatizing the conquest of Death by the Redeemer. Bryant had, incidentally, preferred Blair to Porteus; he cited the "superior originality in thought and vigor of expression" of "the finer passages" in "The Grave."[3]

The presumptive evidence is strong that one of these "finer passages" from Blair was the following: "What is this world? / What but a specious burial-field unwalled, / Strewed with Death's spoils. . . ."[4] Bryant in "Thanatopsis," referring to the earth as "one mighty sepulchre," was to describe the hills, sea, and other scenic natural objects as "the solemn decorations all / Of the great tomb of man." If Blair's tone had been one of Gothic horror, Bryant's was one of meditative calm. Similarly, in "Death" there are the lines in which Bishop Porteus, lapsing into the heavy irony of the pulpit moralist, had written: "In Fancy's fairy paths / Let the gay songster rove, and gently trill / The strain of empty joy."[5] In "Thanatopsis" the poetic idea becomes:

> . . . The gay will laugh
> When thou art gone, the solemn brood of care

> Plod on, and each one as before will chase
> His favorite phantom; yet all these shall leave
> Their mirth and their employments . . .

Thus, Bryant would derive from verses, which not only were te-
diously didactic but also drew upon clear theological assumptions,
the ingredients for his highly original message. On the one hand,
a metaphor expressing the contempt of orthodox Protestantism for
things of this world is converted to laud the abundant beauty of
nature; on the other, the disdain for frivolous amusement expressed
by Bishop Porteus is muted by placing both gaiety and industry on
the same plane.

But there was another element of Christian thought that made
stronger claims upon Bryant's imagination. Several of his earlier
poems had focused upon the retributive aspects both of death and
of life beyond the grave, and, while Bryant had no vision of a heaven
or hell, the idea that divine will manifested itself through the taking
of life had an undeniable fascination for him. In 1815 he had written
the poem known as "Not That From Life and All Its Woes," in
which the following lines appear:

> There is a sacred dread of death
> Inwoven with the strings of life.
> This bitter cup at first was given
> When angry *justice* frown'd severe,
> And 'tis th' eternal doom of heaven
> That man must view the grave with fear.[6]

Bryant's "Hymn to Death" (1820) subjects this idea to its crucial
test. Death is glorified throughout the early portions of the blank
verse as a "Deliverer" appointed by God "to free the oppressed /
And crush the oppressor." Although men have slandered Death,
naming him the "king of terrors," an "assassin," or "the spoiler of
the world," the poet asserts that "I am come to speak / Thy praises."
But the poet's excesses were cruelly corrected before he had completed the poem—Dr. Peter Bryant had died:

> Alas! I little thought that the stern power,
> Whose fearful praise I sang, would try me thus
> Before the strain was ended. It must cease—

> For he is in his grave who taught my youth
> The art of verse . . .
>
> . . . Shuddering I look
> On what is written, yet I blot not out
> The desultory numbers; let them stand,
> The record of an idle revery.[7]

This poem reveals Bryant at his experimental best, seeking for the tone and argument that he could finally accept among a variety of alternatives.

From its inception, "Thanatopsis" moved in a radically different direction from that which visualized Death as an agent of divine retribution. But even in "Thanatopsis," in a fugitive passage that was soon stricken from the manuscript, the complementary doctrine of divine mercy was alluded to: "By the kind hope that mercy will accept / Perfect the imperfect duties of thy life / And pardon all thy errors. . . ."[8] Only the tightest discipline kept his perspective and subject directly before the poet. The moral assumptions of Christianity were, in large part, his assumptions also.

Contrasts with Sentimental Attitudes

However, there were poetic visions of death other than those based upon orthodox Christianity. As Carl Van Doren pointed out more than seventy years ago, "Thanatopsis" was an answer to the frantic questioning of the poetry of Henry Kirke White, a British poet of the late eighteenth century. Bryant's response to Kirke White's morbid lyrics was, as remembered in his reminiscences, enthusiastic: "I read the [*The Remains of Kirke White*] with great eagerness, and so often that I had committed several of them to memory, particularly the ode to Rosemary. The melancholy tone which prevails in them deepened the interest with which I read them, for about that time I had, as young poets are apt to have, a liking for poetry of a querulous cast."[9]

Van Doren rightly commented that the young Bryant had taken the deeply wounded question of Kirke White, "Who will hear of Henry?" more closely to heart than he had the pat affirmations of religion.[10] He imitated this poet's neurotic apprehensiveness in such lines as "The cold clods press thy limbs above, / The darkness and the worm are there."[11] And he located with even greater precision

than Kirke White did the source of their common anxiety in an
overconscious subjectivity:

> They taught me, and it was a fearful creed
> That God forgets his creatures in the grave
> And to the eternity of darkness leaves
> Thought and its organs. Fearful upon my heart
> Fastened the terrible doubt—and the strong fear
> Of death o'ermastered me . . .
>
> And all that I had learnt of virtue here
> In the world's suffering—all that studious toil
> Had taught me—all that from the book
> Of Nature I had striven to transcribe
> Into my mind—and from the laid-up thoughts
> Of men of other days had now no place—
> Parted—blotted out forever. . . .[12]

Even allowing for some youthful posturing, these lines cast considerable light on the final version of "Thanatopsis," and they explain
the urgency of the fears—for which Nature would have a rebuttal—
in the introductory passage:

>   . . . When thoughts
> Of the last bitter hour came like a blight
> Over thy spirit, and sad images
> Of the stern agony, and shroud, and pall,
> And breathless darkness, and the narrow house,
> Make thee to shudder, and grow sick at heart. . . .

Not the concern for eternal life, nor the prospect of damnation
motivated these lines. The problem was one for natural man alone
to face and to resolve without the palliatives of religion. How was
the autonomous mind to accept its annihilation?

If Bryant drew part of "Thanatopsis" from a poetry of questioning
despair, he drew another part from a poetry of facile assertion. The
conception of Nature as a maternal figure, implicit throughout the
early lines of the poem, and the language of the final lines are echoes
of a verse by Mrs. Lydia Sigourney—the Sweet Singer of Hartford.
This work, "A Versification of a remark by Pliny," appeared in the
same issue of the *North American Review* as the early version of

"Thanatopsis" (prior to the addition of the pertinent lines), and it is characteristic of a shallow sensibility at work on the same theme. According to Mrs. Sigourney, Earth is distinctive among the various forces in nature. Unlike the hostile elements, Earth sustains man like a mother and provides him "with a couch of rest at his death." In spite of the buffets of life, natural man is not totally forsaken, and the great Mother has her maudlin eye upon him:

> Yes, earth, kind earth, her new-born son beholds
> Spreads a soft shelter, in her robe enfolds,
> Still like a mother kind, her love retains,
> Cheers by her sweetness, with her food sustains,
> Paints her fair flowers to wake his infant smile,
> Spreads out her fruits to sooth his hour of toil. . . .

And, in a final piece of grotesque imagery, the Earth accepts man as a corpse: "She to her arms, her mould'ring son receives, / Sings a low requiem, to her darling birth, / 'Return! thou loved one, to thy parent earth'."[13]

Bryant rejected the sentimental assumptions of Mrs. Sigourney, of course, but he borrowed her images and phrases. The appearance of "sustained and soothed," for example, in "Thanatopsis" connotes no fanciful activity of an improbable Earth but rather the moral and psychological state of one who is about to die. While Mrs. Sigourney's poem relies upon an easy acceptance of a benevolent nature, Bryant comes to terms with a number of hard facts about human life. Whether or not he was entirely successful in this instance of literary borrowing is, however, an open question. For some critics, these maternal and tranquilizing connotations are never fully integrated into the hard, stoic message of the poem as a whole. Does Nature speak with two voices, one philosophical and one sentimental? The issue is central to any critical assessment of "Thanatopsis," as our subsequent discussion of the poem's meaning and structure will indicate.

Career of "Thanatopsis" through Its Revisions

But first the curious sequence of events that brought about this synthetic poem should be considered. Upon certain of these events, present knowledge is incomplete, but the broad outline is reasonably clear. When Bryant was twenty-one and completing his study of the law, the topic of death powerfully stimulated his imagination. He not only had been reading Kirke White and the other poets of a "querulous cast," but he also had experienced a suicide in his neighborhood, the death of the bride of one of his close friends, and the severe illness which had struck both the poet and his father during the winter of 1814–15. All of these had induced speculative thought on the brevity of human life. During this period Bryant composed several poems about death, including not only "Not That from Life, and All Its Woes," but also "A Chorus of Shades," the latter of which contains a number of images similar to those of "Thanatopsis." Furthermore, the influence of his reading in Wordsworth had begun to manifest itself by 1814 in the pastoral subject matter of his poems and in the relaxation of the iambic stress in his blank verse. It seems reasonably certain that, as Professor William Cullen Bryant II has argued in an excellent article, the first version of "Thanatopsis" in blank verse was composed about 1815.[14]

The next stage in the poem's development was its publication in the September 1817 issue of the *North American Review,* a relatively new periodical edited by those whom Dr. Peter Bryant considered the "literati" of Boston. Dr. Bryant had been urging his son, then a busy, young lawyer, to submit his poetry to the *Review,* but by the summer of 1817 Cullen had shown no inclination to do so. Taking matters in his own hands, the doctor copied several poems his son had left in a desk and took them to Willard Phillips, a friend of long-standing and one of the editors of the journal. Richard Henry Dana, another member of the original board, is supposed to have read these poems with such amazed admiration that he momentarily doubted that they could have been composed by anyone on this side of the Atlantic.[15] Two poems were immediately published in the September issue—"Thanatopsis" and "Not That From Life and All Its Woes"—and two others appeared subsequently— "Inscription for the Entrance to a Wood" and "To a Waterfowl."

In addition to its being rushed into print before its author had completed it to his satisfaction, "Thanatopsis" suffered two further accidents in the process of publication. The first has already been commented upon: the proximity in the issue of Mrs. Sigourney's verse on a similar subject. The second, which has puzzled generations of critics, was the printing of the four rhymed quatrains known as "Not That From Life, and All Its Woes" as an introduction to the blank verse. Perhaps Dr. Bryant had copied both poems on a single page, or perhaps the editors, noting that both poems were literally "about death," saw nothing wrong in combining the regular and blank verses. In either case, Cullen Bryant must have been struck by the obvious conflict between the attitudes toward death conveyed by these quite different poems, and yet he may also have noticed the appropriateness of providing the blank verse with some sort of introduction. These are merely conjectures, but it is significant that the poet, shortly afterward, took up the problem of revising "Thanatopsis" along these two same lines. The subsequent revisions progressed toward a firm refutation of the theme of "Not That From Life and All Its Woes" expressed in the lines: "And 'tis th' eternal doom of heaven / That man must view the grave with fear." And each revision attempted to introduce "Thanatopsis" in such a way that the consolations for death emanated from a single identified source.

Bryant's central problem as he revised his poem was this matter of the source of his consolations. And yet the structure of his poetic method clearly limited the alternative sources of his "voice"; there were only two parties to the poet's dialogue with Nature. Either the speaker had to be man himself—obviously the most interested party—or it had to be nature, who was, perhaps too disinterested. On the other hand, what was there about the relationship between man and nature that qualified either participant in the dialogue to speak on this crucial matter, much less to offer compelling consolations? The dilemma was unavoidable. At last the young poet had struck upon material that resisted his talent and challenged his philosophical outlook. The two subsequent revisions, the second of which became the final text, groped toward both truth and form.

In the nine lines that begin the revision of 1818–20 (designated as Manuscript B by McDowell[16]), the consolation emanates from the "better genius" of the poet. Nature acts merely as a catalyst, reminding man of his mortality. But the dialogue itself is internal and introspective, as the higher faculties of the poet spout philosophy to the mortal flesh.

These nine lines had been—possibly—part of the earlier manuscript and thus their appearance in Manuscript B may be no more than the young poet's refusal to acknowledge the editorial tampering (by his father?) that had prevented their appearance in the *Review*. But whether the lines were, about 1818, being salvaged from an earlier version, or whether, in the poet's conception of his work,

they had never been deleted, they were still a meaningful option to
him up to those months of 1821 that he spent in Cambridge preparing his poetry for the first volume of collected works.

The possibility that these following lines were rejected as inferior
verse cannot be overlooked, particularly if Dr. Bryant had found
them wanting. Their diction, imagery, and rhythms are, however,
quite consistent with "Thanatopsis" as a whole; and it seems unlikely
that Bryant would have discarded such potentially rich material in
its entirety unless their controlling idea was inadequate.

> It was his better genius that was wont
> To steal upon the bard what time his steps
> Sought the repose of nature, lone and still
> And unfrequented walks—and in his ear
> To whisper things of which it irks the mind
> That clings to the dead fallacies of life
> To think:—and gravely with his graver hours
> Oft the benevolent and heedful one
> Would thus commune——

What was it that made the voice of the "better genius" unac-
ceptable to Bryant? Several alternatives suggest themselves. First
was the undisguised subjectivity and implied intuitionism of this
approach, which stressed those elements of imported romanticism
least attractive to the American reader. Even twenty years later,
Emerson's appeal to the "genius" latent within all men was to fall
upon hostile ears, if heard at all. Throughout Bryant's poetry, the
interior life is corrected by the exterior life, or, at the very least,
the racial life anterior to the individual. Although Bryant would
share with Emerson an antipathy to certain kinds of authority and
although he reserved the right to question the "truths" imposed
upon him by reality, he was never to grasp the full implications of
the doctrine of self-reliance. Indeed, his very use of the idea of
"better genius" in these lines is less transcendental than Byronic,
more introspective than intuitive.

Yet even the introspective tone had its weakness, quite apart from
the philosophical implications. For, as Bryant might well have recognized, this is the tone of self-pity and of egotistic anxiety. Nature's
solitude and beauty relieved men of their low view of life and
introduced an element of the sublime into even the most prosaic
activities and thoughts. Thus it was inappropriate, and perhaps

actually insensitive, for the poet to seek the repose and stillness of nature, only so that he might better hear his own voice, as, indeed this earlier version of the poem has it. And a further but less significant objection to the "better genius" is that it left Bryant without any meaningful conclusion to his poem. Given his lack of full confidence in the inner voice, the problem of resolving its dilemmas in any suitable artistic fashion was nearly impossible. Though he tried to make the consolations stick—in one draft by reasserting the universality of death, in the other by a last minute assertion of Christian sentiments—there was lacking the firmness and formal strength that consolations, if they are to succeed at all, must have.

The Voice of Nature

If such difficulties lay in this direction, why did not Bryant immediately seize upon the other alternative? Why did he delay for five years before making the consolations spring from the voice of Nature? The answer to these questions is suggested by the contrast between "Thanatopsis" and the poetic effort of Mrs. Sigourney. The danger that nature might be reduced to human proportions through such personifications as that of Mrs. Sigourney was even greater than the danger of subjectivism. Nature was, by Bryant's unspoken definition, the great movement of time through all the transient phenomena of the material world. That nature, so defined, should concern itself with the passing of consciousness was not immediately plausible, for what is consciousness but the perception of the phenomenal flux? Nature as environment, no matter how sublimely conceived, would have no consolations for the minor discomforts that its great work may have occasioned. Only the sentimentalist could detect in the murmur of this magnificent machine any acknowledgment of man's significance in the scheme of things.

We cannot know that Bryant considered the problem of revision in exactly these terms, but his alterations show him as first choosing nature as his voice, and then going a step further than was his usual practice in establishing the philosophical base upon which his poem was to be founded. Nature was more than environment; nature becomes, in Baudelaire's famous phrase, *un forêts de symboles*. The dialogue of the poet was not merely with his environment but with the "visible forms" through which a higher wisdom is communicated. In "Thanatopsis," as in no other poem, Bryant was driven to recognize that his poetic dialogue was no simple dialectic between subject-Man and object-Nature; it was instead an involved process of creation in which physical objects and poetic images were not easily distinguishable. That nature might itself project a metaphorical language, no better than the vision that changes its focus from one poem to the next, was the unique realization of "Thanatopsis": "To him who in the love of Nature holds / Communion with her visible forms, she speaks / A various language. . . ."

Throughout the poem this emphasis upon the differences between "forms" and some sort of transcendent reality reoccurs. The "pale form" of line 20 and the "fair forms" of line 36 both refer to the material remains—the corpse of the poet. The sufferings of a dying man are, as conceived by the poet, "sad images." In line 64 human beings are described in terms that connote the illusory quality of life: ". . . and each one as before will chase / His favorite phantom. . . ." And the concluding statement of the poem, which occurs only in the final draft, defines decisively the limited role of visual perceptions, whether they be "forms," "images," "phantoms," or, as in this case, "pleasant dreams": " . . . approach thy grave, / Like one who wraps the drapery of his couch / About him, and lies down to pleasant dreams."

In contrast to the aberrations of sight, however, are the verities of sound. Not the sounds of sense perception, it is true, but the mysterious words that the Old Testament prophets had heard emerging out of the burning bushes and whirlwinds of their symbolic surroundings. Like Grey before him and Tennyson after,[17] Bryant seized upon the provocative paradox of the "still voice," and in the context of "Thanatopsis" made it a credible source of his consolations for death. For the poet as listener, in contrast to the poet as seeker or visionary, was all that the poem needed. The dialogue was maintained, albeit somewhat onesidedly, and the vastness of nature was not diminished through a trivial metaphor. Bryant could have his visual imagery, yet deny it, too, as the very lines in which the still voice occurs demonstrate:

> Go forth, under the open sky, and list
> To Nature's teachings, while from all around—
> Earth and her waters, and the depths of air—
> Comes a still voice—

The power and meaning of "Thanatopsis" hang by this slender thread. Rational consciousness and natural piety are both satisfied by this simple, allusive device. The dialogue, seemingly threatened by the absorption of consciousness into the perpetual cycle of nature, has been restored on a deeper level of understanding than that implied by the other poems of nature. For the assumption upon which all of the consolations of the poem are based is that the faculty of human reason—while it may operate independently of nature and achieve a degree of self-realization—can never enter into a dialogue with Nature on equal terms. That Nature speaks to a man through forms—including his own "pale form"—and with a "various language" indicates the limitations of human understanding. Indeed, it is this insight, with its suggestion of Hebraic prophecy, that motivates the entire development of the theme of "Thanatopsis." The human reason is gently persuaded to abandon its presumptuous claims to uniqueness and autonomy. Death is to be recognized as a fulfillment of the life of partial knowledge—not as the termination of an absolute consciousness. The dialogue no longer assumes that the voice of man is capable of bouncing echoes off an objective mountain; it proceeds in the understanding that the very images, words, sounds, and ideas projected by man are merely chips and slivers from a monumental wholeness and truth. Although the dialogue is still functional in the poem, the poet at last has been awed into a tentative silence while the "still voice" of universal wisdom has its say.

Sermon as Structure

However, this reversal—or inversion—of the customary direction of the dialogue posed formal problems even while it solved intellectual ones. The blank verse could no longer drift on the currents of the poet's reverie. The poet could no longer apostrophize and interrogate, as he had in "To a Waterfowl." Nor could he turn inward upon his personal experience, as he had, for example, in "The Yellow Violet." On the contrary, the formal requirements were, first, a clear progression of ideas toward a definitive conclusion; second, a calm, authoritative voice that spoke not merely to the poet in his privacy but to all receptive men; and third, a language that would apply universal truth to the commonplace.

Each of these requirements had been met by a rhetorical style that Bryant, throughout his youth, had encountered sabbath after sabbath. The old "plain style," imported to New England by the earliest settlers, had been preserved in the small towns of white clapboard houses through nearly two centuries of theological strife. And the sermon in the plain style was as eminently lucid as the village steeple in its architectural development, unmistakably structured according to a tripartite division into *doctrine, reason,* and *uses.*[18] Its voice was that of the chosen man of God who applied his gifts to further explanation of God's word as revealed in scripture. Its language was simple and homely. In the words of Thomas Hooker it would "make a hard point easy and familiar in explication."[19] Although Bryant may not have been aware that the plain-style sermon was the form he sought, its applicability was clear enough. Consciously or not, "Thanatopsis" became a romantic sermon.

The division of the poem into three parts is clearly indicated by the stanzaic patterns. The first section (through line 30) establishes, in lieu of revealed truth, the authority of Nature as it speaks through the "still voice" and as it offers the "doctrine" that man is to lose "each human trace." The second section (lines 31–72), in a close analogy to the *reasons* by which the Puritan divine would convince his listeners of the rational basis of the *doctrine,* argues persuasively against the objections men raise to their deaths. The third section (lines 73–81) applies the theme of the poem—just as the *uses* of the plain-style sermon had applied the message of the Scripture— to the ordinary course of human life. Like the seventeenth-century divine, Bryant prefaced his rational consideration of the human plight with an appeal to a higher authority, and he concluded it with a direct application to the moral life. This simple, sturdy form—which had brought a vigorous clarity into the religious life of American Protestantism—instilled into "Thanatopsis" its own rugged genius. The indigenous culture of Bryant's native land had contributed, in a fashion unsuspected by either his admirers or his detractors, to the formation of a poetic masterpiece, the first created since the founding of the republic.

As our knowledge of the various stages through which "Thanatopsis" passed clearly shows, the realization of this tripartite form was the final, decisive phase. Only in Cambridge, two and a half years after the poem had appeared in the *North American Review,* did the voice of Nature emerge to state its doctrine, or did the poet recognize that his personal reflections on death had led him to the inescapable moral conclusion of the final lines. The poem expanded almost of its own accord into a readily available form. Although the sermon form was rigid, its adoption was the result of an organic process. The revision of "Thanatopsis" was no mere matter of patching and padding; it was an evolution of thought and feeling toward an ultimate goal. Perhaps the goal was implicit in the language of Manuscript A in the passage evoking the burial of the human body and the loss of sensate functions. Perhaps the argument "Yet not to thine eternal resting place . . ." that we have compared to the *reasons* of the plain-style sermon, demanded a more disciplined framework than that provided by reverie and undirected blank verse. In any case, the successive manuscripts reveal Bryant moving through various alternatives toward a final version of his poem—a version in which thought and form are gracefully united.

Contrasts in Intent and Tone

A recognition of the broad outlines of the Puritan sermon in "Thanatopsis" does more, however, than reveal a subliminal means for achieving this unity in the poem; it defines the specific intent of each of the three sections. The initial passage, as we have seen, introduces the philosophical premises of the poem, as well as the major problem to be resolved. The central section, however, drops from the level of meditation to that of debate. The third and final passage once more elevates the discourse by its direct assault on the moral behavior of man. The possibility of an intentional shift from the second to the third sections—a change of voice from nature to the poet as Professor Arms has asserted—seems dubious from the available evidence; but the shift is, nevertheless, a radical and important one.[20] The appeal of the *reasons* is primarily to the logical faculties and that of the *uses* is principally to the emotions.

The polemic nature of the former appeal is self-evident. The first three lines explicitly state the two points to be debated: the community of the dead and the dignity of natural death—"Yet not to thine eternal resting-place / Shalt thou retire alone, nor couldst thou wish / Couch more magnificent." The community of the dead, an answer to man's fear of the "narrow house," is made clear by a catalog of past members of the race who have succumbed, a reference to contemporary beings who will share this fate, and a reminder that even future generations "Shall one by one be gathered to thy side, / By those, who in their turn shall follow them." The dignity of natural death is asserted as an answer to the humiliation that a gentleman and humanist must feel being "a brother to the insensible rock / And to the sluggish clod, which the rude swain / Turns with his share, and treads upon." The consolations for this indignity, as offered by the "still voice," are persuasive. Those who have gone before are people of virtue and social status: "The powerful of the earth—the wise, the good." And furthermore, all the physical forms of Nature lend beauty and dignity to the grave. The earth, the sea, the planets "Are but the solumn decorations all / Of the great tomb of man." Thus, beneath the swelling cadences of the verse and the moving imagery of this passage lies the groundwork of a developed argument.

The concluding nine lines of the poem, however, with their pervasive muted and sibilant consonants ("silent halls of death" and "lies down to pleasant dreams"), and their surreal images of caravans, silent halls, and draped couches, contain little cognitive thought. Man is enjoined to approach his grave "sustained and soothed / By an unfaltering trust," but he is given no rationale for doing so. Just as the active and conscious mind accepts sleep, so should it submit to a final relaxation. Only the gauche intellect, anxiety-ridden in the midst of the Nature that has produced and nurtured him, would ask "Why?" If the consolations for his sense of isolation and for the prick to his intellectual pride have not sufficed, there is little more that can be said.

One has only to read Elisabeth Kubler-Ross's *On Death and Dying* to become aware of how the movement toward acceptance of death is a final stage, arrived at as the individual approaches the anticipated moment of his or her passing.[21] "Thanatopsis" does not, it is clear, lead one sequentially through all of the four preparatory states of denial and isolation, anger, bargaining, and depression, but it implies or assumes them in its development. The references to "darker musings," "the last bitter hour," "sick at heart," "melancholy waste," and "withdraw / in silence from the living" provide the essential context, the preliminary states of mind and heart, for the ultimate state of acceptance. Bryant had, we can speculate, passed through in his imagination the stages on the way to death and out of this experience had made his master poem.

The hard-won depth and complexity of "Thantopsis" was a tour de force for Bryant, an achievement that his other poems about death were not to equal. A piece titled "The Burial Place" (1818) and subtitled "A Fragment" attempts to develop one of the ideas in "Thanatopsis," but it fails to recognize either the dialogue of man with nature or the resistance of the intellect to death. It is basically a descriptive sketch in blank verse, contrasting the yew-studded, willow-shaded cemeteries of England (which Bryant was not to visit for some years) with the harsh purity of the Yankee burial grounds. Unlike Robert Lowell, who would catch the spirit of Promethean heroism in the graveyard of the seafaring folk of Nantucket, Bryant was to see only "Melancholy ranks of monuments . . . where the coarse grass, between, / Shoots up its dull green spikes. . . ." But, as "Thanatopsis" had also pointed out, nature supplies its own beauty to the graves of mankind:

> Nature, rebuking the neglect of man,
> Plants often, by the ancient mossy stone,
> The brier-rose, and upon the broken turf
> That clothes the fresher grave, the strawberry plant
> Sprinkles its swell with blossoms, and lays forth
> Her ruddy, pouting fruit. . . .[22]

Sympathy for Old World customs was not, of course, characteristic of Bryant. So similar was the description of the English rural burial-place to a passage in Irving's *Sketchbook,* that Bryant felt called upon in the 1832 edition to disclaim any borrowing from that source.

A subsequent poem, "The Two Graves" (1826), takes up another idea from "Thanatopsis," the notion that death is lonely. Whereas "Thanatopsis" had argued that the dead join with others of the race, "The Two Graves" suggests the essential desirability of privacy in death. This reflection is inspired by the poet's recollection of the graves of an old pioneer couple who had been buried near their homestead. On returning to the spot, however, he must come to terms with oblivion:

> Two low green hillocks, two small gray stones,
> Rose over the place that held their bones;
> But the grassy hillocks are levelled again,
> And the keenest eye might search in vain,
> 'Mong briers, and ferns, and paths of sheep,
> For the spot where the aged couple sleep.[23]

This oblivion is not to be lamented. In fact, it is preferable to a common burial ground where the dead are "Crowded, like guests in a banquet-room." The old couple have been permitted to remain near their earthly domicile instead of being "borne to a distant sphere," and the poet fancies that they still linger near the spot, quietly enjoying the sunshine, the music of the brook, and the passing of the seasons. Such sentimental naturalism, quite different from the philosophy of "Thanatopsis," leads the poet to generalize glibly upon the doctrine of the ascension of the soul after death: "Tis a cruel creed, believe it not! / Death to the good is a milder lot."

In "The Two Graves," Bryant lapsed back into the poetic pitfalls that he had skillfully avoided in "Thanatopsis": the easy acceptance of nature as pure benevolence, the unconsidered reliance upon sense experience, the imputation of ethical judgments to death, and the attempt to face the problem of immortality within the framework of nature poetry. The plight of the conscious mind as it contemplates the immediacy of death has been all but forgotten. The emotional and intellectual power that had created "Thanatopsis" had been, in a few short years, dissipated and eventually lost.

The poet, if he sticks to his craft, may postpone important considerations and turn to other subject matter, but permanently dispel them he cannot. In his declining years, mellowed by success and by failure, sobered by the great public events of his time, and confirmed in his worldview, Bryant returned to his theme. Such poems of wisdom as "Among the Trees," "October, 1866," "Tree-Burial," "A Life Time," and "The Flood of Years" lack the lyrical nerve and the intellectual bones of "Thanatopsis," but each seriously considers the meaning of death for the mortal man.

Within the great cycles of history and nature, these poems assert, death operates unfailingly, not as a curse or a judgment, but as evidence of the permanent reality—spiritual and moral—that lie behind the facade of the moment. "Among the Trees" praises the trees as emblems of the permanence of nature that outlives "The flitting generations of mankind."[24] "October, 1866" is an elegy on the poet's wife, three months deceased, in which his sorrow and grief are gradually transcended through a moral awareness of her continuing influence on his life. "Tree-Burial" presents, sympathetically and sanely, the lament of the Indian mother for her child, and it again dwells upon the close ties that bind the living and the dead.

"A Lifetime" picks up the theme once more as the poet—reflecting upon his wife, his youngest child, and the other loved ones who have died—sees their faces above him "In the far blue deeps of air": "And I stretch my arms with transport / From where I stand below." Still he is enough of a moral man to refrain from an overt wish for union with the dead; the vision fades and he is left alone once more:

> I am gazing into the twilight
>   Where the dim-seen meadows lie,
> And the wind of night is swaying
>   The trees with a heavy sigh.[25]

Finally, in "The Flood of Years" these themes are brought together, and the transience of mortal grief is placed in bold relief against the "eternal Change" and "everlasting Concord." The poem concludes with the reuniting of families and loved ones:

> Old sorrows are forgotten now,
> Or but remembered to make sweet the hour
> That overpays them; wounded hearts that bled
> Or broke are healed forever. In the room
> Of this grief-shadowed present, there shall be
> A Present in whose reign no grief shall gnaw
> The heart . . .[26]

Although there is no longer a sense of conflict and discovery and although the verse of these poems tends toward prolixity, the basic insight into the momentary and partial response to experience by rational men still prevails. The qualities of "Thanatopsis" are distinguishable once more in these poems.

Chapter Four
Poems of Progress

Nearly one-fifth of the poems composed by William Cullen Bryant make reference, if only in passing, to political ideas or events. This fact, together with his active career as a journalist, has led many to view him as a sort of poet-publicist—as a commentator on public affairs in verse in the tradition of Phillip Freneau and the Connecticut Wits. The very topicality of such titles as "The Embargo," "The Greek Boy," "The Massacre at Scio," and "The Death of Lincoln" has encouraged this generalization to the point where it threatens to obliterate another very important facet of his work. For not only did Bryant master the medium of public verse, but he also wrote creatively and searchingly on the issues his century brought before him. In his best works he became the seeker of truth, the reconciler of contradictions, the entertainer of doubts and ambiguities. To a lesser extent, perhaps, than in his poems on nature or death, his poems of progress still reveal the responses of the private self to the experience of the world. His powerful visions of human history and natural processes are brought forward to make their comments on the "issues" before him and to contribute toward these integrated and balanced complexes of feelings and ideas that are works of art.

When considered in the light of Bryant's career and personal inclinations, the themes of the political verse are predictable: freedom, the rights of mankind, the nobility of the human spirit, human progress. In this respect the poems differ little from his editorials or his public addresses. Though the editorials are deductive, working rapidly toward specifics from an unexamined premise, and the poems tend to be inductive, starting with an image or an experience and culminating with a general idea, in each form of expression the ideological framework is that of the rationalist and liberal. Even in months of doubt and confusion, the ideals of the early republic still prompted him. Somehow, evidence and experience to the contrary, reasonable men could stand in the center of their environment and direct it toward some higher good. Somehow—all violence, tyranny, greed, and corruption notwithstanding—human society could share

with natural processes the propensity to renew itself and to bring
forth fresh, beautiful forms of life.

The Publicist

This similarity in the structure of Bryant's thought in the poems
and editorials makes necessary some understanding of the man as
publicist and as editor-in-chief of the *Evening Post.* For continuing
commentary on the political and social affairs of the day, newspaper
writing, much more than poetry, provided the better vantage point
and commanded the wider audience. Considering Bryant's aversion
to the rough-and-tumble of active politics, the editorial chair was
indeed a favorable location for him.

This is not to say that he found newspaper work consistently
attractive and agreeable. His personal letters gave voice to minor
complaints of pressure, fatigue, and boredom, but the most telling
statements upon journalism are those made publicly. The first,
which is high-minded and innocent, is from an early article recorded
by Allan Nevins in his book about the *Post*; the second, the somber
and disillusioned one, appeared in 1851 on the twenty-fifth anniversary of Bryant's connection with the daily:

Circa 1830—
   Yet the vocation of a newspaper editor is a useful and indispensable,
and if rightly exercised, a noble vocation. It possesses this essential element
of dignity—that they who are engaged in it are occupied with questions
of the highest importance to the happiness of mankind.[1]
. . . .

November, 1851—
   [Journalism] fills the mind with a variety of knowledge relating to the
events of the day, but that knowledge is apt to be superficial, since the
necessity of attending to many subjects prevents the journalist from thoroughly investigating any. In this way it begets desultory habits of thought,
disposing the mind to be satisfied with mere glances at difficult questions,
and to dwell only upon plausible commonplaces. The style gains by it in
clearness and fluency, but it is apt to become, in consequence of much
and hasty writing, loose, diffuse, and stuffed with local barbarisms and
cant phrases of the day.[2]

This same article of 1851, "Reminiscences of the 'Evening Post',"
made the point that journalism supplies insights into dark and selfish

motives, while it also reveals the "influences" at work in forming public attitudes. Such insight, Bryant explained, creates the temptation "to betray the cause of truth to public opinion," but fortunately the *Evening Post* "has not often yielded."[3] As Nevins's study of the *Post* demonstrates, this boast and the following one by Bryant were both fully warranted:

Its success and its limits to its success may both, perhaps, be owing to the unaccommodating and insubservient quality. It is often called upon, by a sense of duty, to oppose itself to the general feeling of those from whom a commercial paper must receive its support; it never hesitates to do so. It sometimes finds a powerful member of the community occupied with projects which it deems mischievous; it puts itself in his way, and frustrates his designs, if possible.[4]

Liberalism

Such a conception of the role of the journalist goes far in illuminating the attitudes that Bryant, in association with other members of the editorial board of the *Post,* expressed toward the issues of the era. Motivated by that "sense of duty" he mentions, the editorial writer speaks for the public as opposed to the private interest, and, through his attack on inequities, he hopes to maintain a stable, democratic social order. A curious negativism in Bryant's position upon many of the great matters that concerned him arises out of his assumption that progress is on the side of mankind and flourishes best when events are allowed to flow without obstruction. His reading in his young manhood in the political economists— Smith, Say, Thornton, and Ricardo—had confirmed in him his conception of the healthy society as one in which the unregulated flow of goods and payments seeks its proper state of equilibrium. What in the economic sphere was the posture of laissez-faire became in matters of primarily social import a militant desire for freedom and a distrust of artificial restraints.

Even in the decade of Reconstruction, Bryant was able to recollect the events he had witnessed and to discern the signs of continuing improvement in the state of mankind—not because of arbitrary systems or through the intervention of government, but through a kind of enlargement of the sensibilities of people within a relatively free and fluid environment:

I have lived long, as it may seem to most people, however short the term appears to me when I look back upon it. In that period have occurred various most important changes, both political and social, and on the whole I am rejoiced to say that they have, as I think, improved the condition of mankind. The people of civilized countries have become more enlightened, and enjoy a greater degree of freedom. They have become especially more humane and sympathetic, more disposed to alleviate each other's sufferings. This is the age of charity. In our day, charity has taken forms unknown to former ages, and occupied itself with the cure of evils which former ages neglected.[5]

This social philosophy, which would find one kind of articulation in the poetry, also provided definite "principles" available to the besieged writers of editorials. As he would break down the tariff barriers, so would he oppose the creation of mercantile monopolies. As he would support the rights of labor to bargain for wages, so would he argue for freedom of the press. In matters where the power of the federal government threatened to create inequities among social classes or sections of the nation—such as through the establishment of the national bank, internal improvements, or in the regulation of currency—his position was that of the strict constructionist of the constitution who advocated severe limitations upon the powers of the federal government. At each point he would resist control by the few in favor of charity toward the many.

In all of those areas, as Godwin observed, Bryant was more practical than doctrinaire. While the notion of an open society colored all of his pronouncements, there was no attempt to impose utopian ideals upon the existing community. Although Godwin might flirt with Fourierism and back the enterprise of the transcendentalists at Brook Farm and although Leggett—during his short-lived tenure as editor in Bryant's absence—was to wage an immoderate assault on the commercial establishment of New York City, Bryant's strength lay in his willingness to accept the restraints of meliorism. To Emerson, he appeared to be a "historical" democrat, who was "interested in dead or organized, but not in organizing liberty."[6] Among the radicals, his acceptance of social norms seemed at times like conservatism, just as his liberal attitude toward the adjustment of the norms for the public good seemed like radicalism to the Whigs. But through all factional disputes he remained aloof, tending to keep the *Post* as free as possible from the extremes of both radicalism and reaction.

In regard to slavery, the topic of greatest controversy in his day, his position clung closely to liberal principles even while he faced the complexities of crises. When Garrison's *Liberator* brought the attention of the nation to Abolition in 1832, the *Post* was silent, but Bryant had expressed as early as 1820 his hostility toward slavery. Bryant and his editors, consistent with the liberal view, imagined that slavery was doomed to extinction because of its anomalous place in a democratic society. But the wave of reaction instigated by the alliance of Southern slave holders and Northern merchants—the censorship of the mails; the martyrdom of Lovejoy; the move to annex Texas as a nucleus for a slave-holding empire in the West; and, ultimately, those twin horrors, the Fugitive Slave Law and the Missouri Compromise—all of these were clearly anathema to the proponent of a free society. While rival New York newspapers joined with the Washington *Globe* in denouncing the *Post,* Bryant supported the right of the Abolitionists to be heard: "We are resolved that the subject of slavery shall be, as it ever has been, as free a subject for discussion, as the difference between whiggism and democracy, or the differences between Arminians and Calvinists."[7] Such was the position that distinguished the *Post* from the *Emancipator,* which made Bryant a Free Soiler and, later, a Republican, rather than an Abolitionist.

Indeed, it was the moderate position of the *Post,* its opposition to any extension of slavery into the territories but its acquiescence in the predicted demise of the "peculiar institution" through natural causes where it then existed, that formed the rallying point for the Republican party. Only when secession was an unavoidable fact did Bryant advocate the exertion of federal power, but once Fort Sumter had been bombarded, he fully recognized the necessity for the preservation of the Union at all costs. His criticism of Lincoln's administration was directed only toward inefficiency and ineffectiveness in military affairs; he was in firm agreement with the objectives of the war.

In other areas also the same staunch regard for principle, mixed with a healthy concern for expeditious action, was characteristic of the *Post* under Bryant's leadership. He backed reform efforts for the creation of a more humane penal system, for the abolition of capital punishment, and for the strengthening of laws regarding criminal carelessness and manslaughter. To the problem of corruption, which had overtaken the many branches of the government during the

Civil War, Bryant and Godwin brought a vigorous campaign for civil service reform. Closer to Bryant's personal interests, but less successful as a crusade, was the program for an international copyright. In the 1820s he had formed a common cause on this issue with Benjamin Coleman, the founder of the *Post,* and, in the 1840s, he was to report in detail the acid comments of Charles Dickens on this topic during his American tour. At many levels of social and governmental activity, in great matters and small, Bryant raised the persuasive voice of reason: arguing for equity and justice even while maintaining a wary eye toward what he considered to be dangerous concentrations of power.

Bryant realized, as every experienced publicist must, that the inconsistencies of his position were best left unexamined. To suggest that human reason could offer less than perfect solutions to problems essentially insolvable, or to imply that power itself, in spite of its oppressive and injurious features, was the agent of human progress would be to shake the foundations of the editorial appeal for action. For it was toward results—the crystallization of public opinion, agitation, legislation—that Bryant's prose pieces were directed. To the poems were left speculations, questions, and the incompleted cycles of thought. Thus, to the poems were delegated the loose ends and the unclassified images inappropriate for concentrated appeals on the editorial page.

The Public Voice

Before assuming his role as publicist, Bryant had tested the possibilities of combining the critical and poetic functions. Both "The Embargo" (1808) and "The Ages" (1821) represent trials of this sort, and both illustrate the weaknesses inherent in such a combination. As documents for the historian of culture, they are very valuable, yielding insights into the body of opinion that brought New England to the brink of secession in the Hartford Convention of 1814 and the subsequent relaxation of the Federalists in the "Era of Good Feeling." They are less useful, however, as profiles of the poet's thought. Even though the key problems occur in these poems and initiate important lines of development, their treatment is conventional and pedestrian. They are poems in the public voice that make the concessions necessary to unified opinions, and only in occasional lines does the inward voice dare to suggest its presence.

"The Embargo" was the juvenile satire in which Dr. Peter Bryant had taken such an active interest. It expressed the horror and bitterness of the commercial aristocracy of New England, who watched the decline of the mercantile economy brought about—so they supposed—by Jefferson's decree prohibiting further trade with Great Britain. The poem was cast in the mold of the epideictic verse that had flourished during the Revolution and that had reached its highest point of development in the work of Dwight, Trumbull, and the other Connecticut Wits. Structured on the models of classical rhetoric, "The Embargo," like its predecessors, moves through the formal divisions of the exordium, the narration, the proof, the disproof, and the peroration.[8] Consistent also with the genre was the immoderate abuse of the scoundrel, Jefferson, and the exalted praise of Washington as the just and reasonable man. Though its bellicose tone and melodramatic imagery would have led the mature Bryant, even if he had retained his Federalist sympathies, to repudiate "The Embargo," in 1808 it was a considerable achievement for a prospective poet, and it brought him the approval of his father's friends as well as kind words from a reviewer in the *Monthly Anthology*.

The central argument of this poem, submerged as it is at times through the 245 lines, is of some interest in the light of Bryant's later concerns. His proposition is stated in the following lines, which can also serve as an illustration of the rhetoric and tone of the public voice:

> Oh, ye bright pair, the blessing of mankind!
> Whom time has sanction'd, and whom fate has join'd,
> COMMERCE, that bears the trident of the main,
> and AGRICULTURE, empress of the plain;
> Who, hand in hand, and heav'n-directed, go
> Diffusing gladness through the world below;
> Whoe'er the wretch, would hurl the flaming brand,
> Of dire disunion, palsied be his hand!
> Like 'Cromwell damn'd to everlasting fame,'
> Let unborn ages execrate his name!
> Dark is the scene, yet darker prospects threat,
> And ills may follow unexperienc'd yet!
> Oh Heaven! defend, as future seasons roll,
> This western world from Buonoparte's control,
> Preserve our *Freedom,* and our rights secure,
> While truth subsists, and virtue shall endure![9]

The harmonious functioning of Commerce and Agriculture under the direction of heaven was threatened, so runs the young Bryant's thought, because of the divisive action of the unprincipled chief executive. Jefferson's intrusion into the natural workings of the economy, moreover, foreshadows even worse threats to freedom. In the Federalist imagination, the specter of Napoleon and his tyranny loomed large, and Bryant rattles its chains frequently and loudly. For his efforts to maintain peace with Napoleon and for the purchase of the Louisiana Territory, Jefferson is caricatured as "the *willing vassal* of imperious France." For his appeal for support to the democratic masses, Jefferson is described as a "supple" demagogue who lies and flatters in order to secure "each blockhead's vote."

The poem has its happier sentiments, however; for, once "the deep laid plot" is uncovered and the "pirate Gaul" repelled, a new era is in the offing with prosperity for both merchant and yeoman. In the following lines, prophesying the cheerful future, appears the first hint of the idea of progress in Bryant's verse:

> Then on safe seas the merchant's barque shall fly,
> Our waving flag shall kiss the polar sky;
> On canvas wings our thunders shall be borne,
> Far to the west, or tow'rd the rising morn;
> Then may we dare a haughty tyrant's rage,
> And gain the blessings of an unborn age.
>
> 'Tis done, behold the cheerful prospects rise!
> And splendid scenes the startled eye surprise;
> Lo! busy commerce courts the prosperous main;
> And peace and plenty glad our shores again!
> Th' industrious swain sees nature smile around
> His fields with fruit, with flocks, his pastures crown'd.

But though the communal idea is portrayed in vivid colors, in only one short passage of the peroration does the voice of the boy—sensitive to natural imagery and ambitious to prove himself among men—express itself, and then indirectly, in a figure intended to describe the outgrowth of a new nation from the old:

> Thus in a fallen tree, from sprouting roots,
> With sudden growth, a tender sapling shoots,
> Improves from day to day, delights the eyes

> With strength and beauty, stateliness and size,
> Puts forth robuster arms, and broader leaves,
> And high in air, its branching head upheaves.

If the doctrine of progress is only implicit in "The Embargo," obscured, as it were, behind partisan sword-rattling and neoclassical drapery, in "The Ages" (1821) the concept becomes offensively explicit. Although "The Ages" was not issued in pamphlet form, as "The Embargo" had been, in order to disseminate a particular political viewpoint, it is, nonetheless, as carefully directed toward a particular audience and as much a vehicle of communal belief as "The Embargo" itself. Its delivery to the Phi Beta Kappa Society at Harvard College, its subsequent publication in Cambridge by Hillard and Metcalf, and its wide, if not enthusiastic, acceptance by the public as a significant production by the leading American poet are all signs of the poem's limitations as well as indications of its strength.

A piece of illuminating correspondence regarding Bryant's composition of the poem, unearthed and analyzed by C. I. Glicksberg, tends to confirm the impression of the poem received by the reader. The problem, as seen by Bryant's correspondent, was whether to deliver a classical or a pathetic oration—that is, whether the audience should be stirred largely by the weight of accumulated rational argument or by a direct appeal to the sensibilities. But, the advice ran on to say, matters of political concern were best avoided.[10] The stricture was timely, and Bryant, in deference to the Era of Good Feeling, carefully refrained from commentary on the contemporary political scene. That his composition combined both classical and pathetic elements, leaning toward the pathetic, was, however, less significant than that this would be the last time he would compose a lengthy poem to suit the public temper on a particular occasion.

Although the bland optimism of the poem should have been inescapable for any reader, all editions of the work were accompanied by a note which describes its contents and explains its simple purpose: "In this poem, written and first printed in the year 1821, the author has endeavored, from a survey of the past ages of the world, and of the successive advances of mankind in knowledge, virtue, and happiness, to justify and confirm the hopes of the philanthropist for the future destinies of the human race."[11]

What is omitted from this statement about the poem's message is that the philanthropist must look toward the continental United States for the realization of his "hopes." The provincialism of the poem is inescapable, from the Unitarian references to Christ ("The light of hope, the leading star of love,"), through the rejection of the medieval church ("Horrible forms of worship, that, of old / Held, o'er the shuddering realms, unquestioned sway"), to the celebration of Boston harbor ("yon bright blue bay," where "Lifts the white throng of sails, that bear or bring / The commerce of the world").

The basis for the poet's optimism is the growth of human liberty, made possible by the new natural environment of the North American continent. That the human personality has its own inherent determinisms, as Edwards had recognized in his polemic on *Free Will,* or that the natural order imposes a discipline upon all human action, as Emerson was to proclaim in his essay, "Fate," were considerations easily overlooked in Bryant's paean to freedom. In the concluding three stanzas he uses the image of the fetter, or shackles, to suggest the quality of liberty he has in mind—the release from bondage of the prisoner or slave:

> Here the free spirit of mankind, at length,
> Throws its last fetters off; and who shall place
> A limit to the giant's unchained strength,
> Or curb his swiftness in the forward race?
> On, like the comet's way through infinite space,
> Stretches the long untravelled path of light,
> Into the depths of ages; we may trace,
> Afar, the brightening glory of its flight,
> Till the receding rays are lost to human sight.[12]

In spite of its gloomy history of oppression, Europe, too, has hope:

> Europe is given a prey to sterner fates,
> And writhes in shackles; strong the arms that chain
> To earth her struggling multitude of states;
> She too is strong, and might not chafe in vain
> Against them . . .
>   . . . the moment set
> To rescue and raise up, draws near—but is not yet.

But Americans have only the "fetters" of abundance, and the wildness of nature provides an ample shield against aggression:

> But thou, my country, thou shalt never fall,
> Save with thy children—thy maternal care,
> Thy lavish love, thy blessings showered on all—
> These are thy fetters—seas and stormy air
> Are the wide barrier of thy borders, where,
> Among thy gallant sons who guard thee well,
> Thou laugh'st at enemies: who shall then declare
> The date of thy deep-founded strength, or tell
> How happy, in thy lap, the sons of men shall dwell?

As conventional as it is, this image of the "fetters" transmits its
quota of feeling and idea. For a nation with the memory of revolution
still as vivid as the stench of gunpowder, no further development
of the notion was necessary. The ringing indictment of tyranny
contained in the Declaration of Independence is implicit in each
line of such a poem as "The Ages," and the critic who would seek
the depths of its meaning should turn to the militant oratory of the
later decades of the eighteenth century. Though Bryant was not
deeply involved in his theme—indeed, he wrote a friend that composing this poem had made him "sick"—he understood his audience
well. [13] His measured rhetoric, his appeals to the pathetic impulses,
and his descriptive vagueness—all these meet the purposes of the
occasion.

The generation he addressed, those Harvard graduates of 1821,
were of the epigoni, arriving too late on the scene of history to play
heroic roles in either of the two wars against Great Britain. For
Emerson, as for other young men in that audience, the problem of
the past was crucial indeed. And if Emerson's major theme in his
early works was "The sun shines today also," this was not to deny
the urgency of Bryant's vision of the progress of freedom but only
to reassert it with a new emphasis. Emerson no less than Bryant
invoked the spirit of freedom and found its epitome in the development of the American republic. His appeal went further and
deeper than Bryant's, of course, for Emerson searched out the hidden
resources of intellect and spirit in democratic man, but the motivation was directed by the same general cultural predicament. The
old cries of "Liberty," which had once been calls to the standard,
had to be translated into a social philosophy of reform than of violent

action. Thus, in a sense, what "Nature" and "The American Scholar" were to the generation of the late 1830s, "The Ages" was to that of the early 1820s.

Poems of Revolution

Bryant was to abandon this type of massive statement upon his removal to New York, and the poems of the 1820s with political implications tend to be sharper in focus and more explicit in their sympathies. Like many Americans, Bryant was deeply stirred by the conflict in Greece. The situation of the Greek patriots who were attempting to rid their homeland of the Turkish oppressors was too similar to that of the Minutemen of 1776 to be overlooked, and the signs suggested that the forces of Liberty were at work once more. Bryant's contribution to public sentiment was largely poetic (he was editing quarterlies and had not yet joined the *Post*), and it consisted of several lyrical profiles of the Greek heroes.

Representative of these poems, though perhaps more subtle than "The Greek Amazon" (1824) or "The Greek Partisan" (1825), was "The Greek Boy" (1826, 1827). The boy, Evangelides, was an actual public figure in New York at the time. The press had given him considerable publicity, and his likeness was painted in oils by the prominent artist, Robert E. Weir. Subsequently engraved, this portrait, accompanied by Bryant's poem, appeared in *The Talisman* of 1826. The portrait tries to suggest the heritage of the classical past as it lingers in the boy's calm features, and the poem, explicit in its praise for his "martial form," finds hope for the future in one whose "ears have drunk the woodland strains / Heard by old poets." Evangelides was, for Bryant, a symbol of the regenerative forces at work in society, and the final stanza projects upon Greece that optimism of "The Ages" that had bathed America in its warm glow:

> Now is thy nation free, though late;
>   Thy elder brethren broke—
> Broke, ere thy spirit felt its weight—
>   The intolerable yoke.
> And Greece, decayed, dethroned, doth see
> Her youth renewed in such as thee:
> A shoot of that old vine that made
> The nations silent in its shade.[14]

Yet there was a difference between telling the gallant sons of
Harvard graduating in 1821 to laugh at their enemies and encour-
aging Greek partisans to shed blood for the cause of freedom. This
difference emerges as the central theme of "The Conjunction of
Venus and Jupiter" (1826) as the poet reflects on the portents for
America, and then for Greece, of the approach of these two planets
to one another:

> Emblems of power and beauty! well may they
> Shine brightest on our borders, and withdraw
> Toward the great Pacific, marking out
> The path of empire . . .
> . . . .
>
> . . . Happy days to them
> That wed this evening!—a long life of love,
> And blooming sons and daughters! Happy they
> Born at this hour, for they shall see an age
> Whiter and holier than the past, and go
> Late to their graves. Men shall wear softer hearts,
> And shudder at the butcheries of war,
> As now at other murders.
>
> . . . Hapless Greece!
> Enough of blood has wet thy rocks, and stained
> Thy rivers . . .
> . . . .
>
> . . . In yonder mingling lights
> There is an omen of good days for thee.
> Thou shalt arise from midst the dust and sit
> Again among the nations. Thine own arm
> Shall yet redeem thee.[15]

Certainly the emblems of power and beauty are brightest in the
happy land of America, but are they really omens for Greece? Does
the power of Jupiter really apply to the kind of strength needed to
fight a successful rebellion, or does the beauty of Venus correspond
to the terror and bitterness which motivate men to fight for a new
social order? While the conjunction of the two planets may prompt
a conceit that describes America's "path of empire," there is nothing

in the poem to explain how the liaison between these Roman deities can give "new strength" to the embattled Greek partisans.

Thus, the poet's limitation becomes embarrassingly evident. Although the heroic gesture was for Bryant a literary commonplace and though he had fought by the sides of Achilles and Aeneus, the realities of rebellion were unfamiliar to him. When he promises that "And God and thy good sword shall yet work out, / For thee, a terrible deliverance," it is the conventional rhetoric of the public voice still speaking.

Indeed, in a poem like "To the Apennines" (1835) he envisions the spirit of freedom as something totally removed from the ordinary political trials of men. Turning once more to nature, Bryant finds in the lofty mountains the symbol for his idealistic conception of liberty:

> In [the Apennines] the heart that sighs for freedom seeks
>   Her image; there the winds no barrier know,
> Clouds come and rest and leave your fairy peaks;
>   While even the immaterial Mind, below,
> And Thought, her wingèd offspring, chained by power,
> Pine silently for the redeeming hour.[16]

That the citizens of the Italian states—betrayed, as it seemed to many, by the Congress of Vienna, and even then fermenting with the revolutionary violence that was to lead to eventual reunification—should look to the Apennines as some distant "image" of freedom is both plausible and poetically effective. But the disturbing union in this symbol of beauty and power is still unresolved. The explicit contrast in the poem between the "eternal Peace" of the Apennines and the futile, vicious struggles of the plains below in no way contributes to an understanding of how ideals can become operative within public life. The private voice, however, had at last spoken out, if only to find a greater peace than society can offer.

Spain and its disintegrating empire in South America also caught Bryant's poetic interest. His two poems of the period, "The Damsel of Peru" (1826) and "Romero" (1826, 1829), are two quite different treatments of the problems of revolution. "The Damsel of Peru" depicts a young woman proudly supporting the cause of liberation:

> For she has bound the sword to a youthful
>   lover's side,

And sent him to the war on the day she should
have been his bride. [17]

"Romero" introduces a revolutionary warrior who breaks his sword
and retires to a mountain hideout, awaiting the day "when the spirit
of the land to liberty will bound." Bryant's sympathy for the Spanish
people was intense, and it emerges from these poems as it was also
to be expressed in his editorials in the *Evening Post* supporting Simon
Bolivar and his cause. [18]

"The Fountain"

The drift toward a mature political verse had begun, and in "The
Fountain" (1839) Bryant boldly combined his vision of nature and
his conception of human progress. Something of the "happy land"
lingers in his description of the agrarian society that evolves by the
"fountain" (a woodland spring), but far mightier forces are at work
in the poem than those which make and overthrow mere empires.
No longer is the rise of a national republic central to the cosmic
enterprise, for framing the poem is a terrifying conception of the
mysterious subterranean forces that have created the spring and that
shall, in due time, destroy it. The optimism of Bryant's early faith
in human progress is thus drastically qualified by the discovery of
geological change.

"The Fountain" is a complex poem, and the symbolic use of the
fountain—both as a structural device and as a means for synthesizing
ideas—is one of Bryant's finest achievements in blank verse. Starting
with a simple and prosaic analogy between the emergence of clear,
cool water from "red mould and slimy roots of earth" and the
mysterious ways of God, who brings "from the dark and foul, the
pure and bright," the poet moves quickly into his personal response
to the fountain. His observation of the wild-vine, the spice-bush,
the viburnum, and the chipping sparrow conjures up scenes from
the long history of the fountain: first before the intrusion of man,
and then the "histories that stir the heart / With deeper feeling,"
the days of barbarism, savage warfare, and hunting. From these
dark ages—the poem is rich in the imagery of color and light—
rise the pure and bright waters of an agricultural society:

. . . White cottages were seen
With rose-trees at the windows; barns from which

> Came loud and shrill the crowing of the cock;
> Pastures where rolled and neighed the lordly horse,
> And white flocks browsed and bleated. [19]

With the ascent of civilization, however, the fountain—like Nature itself—becomes less significant to the surrounding life. Eventually it is merely an isolated watering spot for the less established members of the community—the woodsman, the hunter, the soldier—and a place for children to play. Here, too, the unsophisticated couples come:

> . . . At eve,
> When thou wert crimson with the crimson sky,
> Lovers have gazed upon thee, and have thought
> Their mingled lives should flow as peacefully
> And brightly as thy waters.

But here also comes the philosopher to read the great truth, not of human progress, but of "eternal change" within the "eternal order" of the universe:

> . . . Here the sage,
> Gazing into thy self-replenished depth,
> Has seen eternal order circumscribe
> And bound the motions of eternal change,
> And from the gushing of thy simple fount
> Has reasoned to the mighty universe.

This "eternal change" that the poet, as well as the sage, recognized, destroys even as it creates. Although no mention is made of the future for the secure rural community that had grown up near the spring, the concluding lines cryptically imply a dark prophecy. Just as the dynamic processes that had brought clear water out of the bowels of the earth had also given rise to a higher state of culture, so these same processes, which can choke off the water at its source or pollute it in passage, can also demolish the "happy land." This conclusion is left unstated, and the conjectures of the poet are intentionally tentative. The poem's message of doom is muted, and these concluding lines are only a solemn reminder of the natural limits of human progress:

> Is there no other change for thee, that lurks
> Among the future ages? Will not man
> Seek out strange arts to wither and deform
> The pleasant landscape which thou makest green?
> Or shall the veins that feed thy constant stream
> Be choked in middle earth, and flow no more
> For ever, that the water-plants along
> Thy channel perish, and the bird in vain
> Alight to drink? Haply shall these green hills
> Sink, with the lapse of years, into the gulf
> Of ocean waters, and thy source be lost
> Amidst the bitter brine? Or shall they rise,
> Upheaved in broken cliffs and airy peaks,
> haunts of the eagle and the snake, and thou
> Gush midway from the bare and barren steep?

This conception of geologic change—in which no apparent purpose is operative but only immutable and inflexible natural laws—was probably derived, as Donald Ringe has pointed out, from Bryant's reading in *The Principles of Geology* by Sir Charles Lyell.[20] The controversial theory of uniformitarianism, which had been advanced by Lyell and attacked by the conservative wing of Protestantism, had emphasized the consistency of natural causes from past ages to the present in the formation of the surface of the earth. For biblical scholars, the uniformitarian theory argued against any providential intervention in the familiar catastrophes of flood and fire, and, for the pious laymen, it placed God too far back in the eons of creation.

"The Fountain" is notable for its subtle avoidance of these issues, and for its use of the theory for imaginative rather than for polemical purposes. In a subsequent poem, "A Hymn of the Sea" (1842), Bryant was to assure the public that God, even though He had taken up geology, was still in His heaven; but "The Fountain" reveals the private processes of imaginative assimilation at work. None of his poems after this period was to sing quite so jauntily of progress, and the ones that took up the theme were to be more restrained in their prophetic glances into the cloudy future.

By his indirection, Bryant confused those readers who shared the unexamined belief in progress that had been defined by "The Ages" and that was assumed by the editorial policy of the *Evening Post*. Parke Godwin's edition of the poems, for example, contains a long note speculating on the place that "The Fountain"—along with

"The Evening Revery" and "Noon" (other poems of time and change)—was to fill in a projected, but never completed, work on the settlement of the New World.[21] That Bryant should have achieved a greater depth than that suggested by "a series of pictures connected by a narrative of personal adventures" was beyond Godwin's comprehension. Unintentionally, Bryant had achieved the kind of healthy obscurantism that is the fate of the poet who searches deeply into himself. But not until the composition of "The Antiquity of Freedom" (1842) was he able to make the elements of natural beauty, progress, power, and freedom fully cohesive and articulate within his personal vision.

"The Antiquity of Freedom"

This master poem, widely read in its own time and frequently anthologized in our own, manages to balance affirmations against reservations and to check the cryptic tendencies of "The Fountain." In its activism and in its seriousness it represents the matured expression of the poet and the definitive position that he was to take, both personally and publicly, on the problems of social order.

Unlike the other poems of progress, "The Antiquity of Freedom" abandons historical figures and natural objects as unifying devices. Instead, directly out of eighteenth-century verse strides the allegorical figure of "Freedom" ("armed to the teeth"), who contends with other, somewhat theatrical, figures identified as "Power" and "Tyranny." Curiously enough, the cumbersome and archaic quality of the allegory fades under Bryant's warmth and skill, and his purpose of elevating his discourse to a philosophical level, while avoiding topical references, is achieved. The narrative element is reduced to a minimum, the poem is kept fairly brief, and the play of ideas is permitted to dominate the verse.

Both beauty and power are introduced early in the poem. The beauty is that of Nature, and the first twelve lines describe the forest glade in which peace and serenity reside:

> Here are old trees, tall oaks, and gnarlèd pines,
> That stream with gray-green mosses; here the ground
> Was never trenched by spade, and flowers spring up
> Unsown, and die ungathered. It is sweet
> To linger here . . .[22]

The poet is moved by the scene, however, to think "Back to the earliest days of liberty," and immediately he apostrophizes the figure of "Freedom":

> O FREEDOM! thou art not, as poets dream,
> A fair young girl, with light and delicate limbs,
> And wavy tresses gushing from the cap
> With which the Roman master crowned his slave
> When he took off the gyves. A bearded man,
> Armed to the teeth, art thou; one mailèd hand
> Grasps the broad shield, and one the sword; thy brow,
> Glorious in beauty though it be, is scarred
> With tokens of old wars; thy massive limbs
> Are strong with struggling.

This figure of manly strength, of course, though scarred and made strong by trials and experience, has its own "beauty." Through his experiences in the area of public affairs, Bryant had come to terms with the activist creed. No longer the pure and innocent idealist who would dream of freedom as a distant peak or as a fair young maiden, he had come to an acceptance of moral conflict as a principle of political progress. Inadequate, indeed, was a chaste, neoclassic *liberté* in the midst of the harsh struggles of the age. It is even doubtful that Bryant would have accepted the detached colossus on Bedloe's Island as an appropriate symbol for the hard-won freedom he contemplated.

The poem rings with the noise of battle and bristles with the harsh energy of the ancient warrior. Freedom withstands the bolts of Power, and, when he is imprisoned and bound by the chain of oppression

> The links are shivered, and the prison-walls
> Fall outward; terribly thou springest forth,
> As springs the flame above a burning pile,
> And shoutest to the nations, who return
> Thy shoutings, while the pale oppressor flies.

Thus, it is clear, Power must be met with Freedom's own power; the brutal violence of the sword is inseparable from man's progress toward eventual freedom. Whereas "The Conjunction of Venus and Jupiter" had considered the momentary meeting of these two symbols to be fortuitous, "The Antiquity of Freedom" asserts the perpetual fusion of beauty and power within the guise (or concept) of Freedom. The record of human progress thus becomes not the simple pattern depicted in "The Ages" but an evolution directed by men toward the specific goal of liberty. The strong affirmation of an activist creed contained in this poem goes far beyond the enthusiasms of the 1820s, and it deepens our understanding of Bryant's later attitudes toward Lincoln and the Civil War.

The poet also clarifies his position on the extent of human responsibility. Freedom is a cause espoused by man, but not created by him: "Thy birthright was not given by human hands: / Thou wert twin-born with man. . . ." And Tyranny, like Evil in the theology of Protestant liberalism, is merely a negation of Good:

> . . . Tyranny himself
> Thy enemy, although of reverend look,
> Hoary with many years, and far obeyed,
> Is later born than thou; and as he meets
> The grave defiance of thine elder eye,
> The usurper trembles in his fastnesses.

It is on the problem of tyranny and civilization that all but the last eight lines dwell. In the tradition of the natural-rights philosophy, the pristine innocence of free people is threatened by the growth of civilization with its many forms of restraint. Thus, while Freedom has in times past withstood Power and Tyranny, now he must be warned against "subtler" forms of snares and ambush:

> Quaint maskers, wearing fair and gallant forms
> To catch thy gaze, and uttering graceful words
> To charm thy ear; while his sly imps, by stealth
> Twine round thee threads of steel, light thread on thread,
> That grow to fetters; or bind down thy arms
> With chains concealed in chaplets. Oh! not yet
> Mayst thou unbrace thy corslet, nor lay by
> Thy sword; nor yet, O Freedom! close thy lids,
> In slumber; for thine enemy never sleeps,
> And thou must watch and combat till the day
> Of the new earth and heaven.

That a raging Samson should become a Gulliver bound by Lilliputians is, quite naturally, intolerable. Freedom of the noble brow

must—as Bryant well knew—"watch and combat" even in the
modern democratic society to preserve his primal identity.

Such a situation has its heroic qualities, and it is upon these that
the peroration dwells, but underneath runs the deeper dye of irony
and pathos. Must the aged warrior be constantly awake against "fair
and gallant forms"—and even be wary of the very garlands that
signify his victory? The concluding lines are directed toward the
pathos rather than the irony of Freedom's plight, but the insight
into the ambiguities of political theory is present. If Freedom rose
from Nature, why should he not, like man, find respite from his
constant vigilance in the charming solitudes of the forest?

> . . . But wouldst thou rest
> Awhile from tumult and the frauds of men,
> These old and friendly solitudes invite
> Thy visit. They, while yet the forest-trees
> Were young upon the unviolated earth,
> And yet the moss-stains on the rock were new,
> Beheld thy glorious childhood, and rejoiced.

Like "The Fountain," this poem recognizes the context into which
the long fight for human liberty must be placed. The values of
activism are real and substantial, but they must also admit to the
corrective balance of peace and acquiescence. Within the matured
philosophical view, nature and society, contemplation and service,
rest and conflict are all elements of the higher order.

Calls to the Standard

After the publication of *The Fountain and Other Poems* (1842),
Bryant wrote no other poems that performed the synthetic function
of "The Fountain" or of "The Antiquity of Freedom." The poems
in the volume titled *The Little People of the Snow* (1863), as Godwin
explained, provided a release for the poet from "the horrors of war"
through escapist fantasies.[23] There were, however, more militant
calls to the standard: "O Mother of a Mighty Race" (1846) was a
defiant protest against Britain's flaunting of American interests in
the boundary disputes in Aroostook County and Oregon.[24] In the
months following the disheartening failure of the Union forces at
the First Battle of Bull Run, Bryant published two poems in the
New York *Ledger,* intended to stiffen Northern resolve to pursue

the war: "Our Country's Call" (1861) and "Not Yet" (1861). Then, at the close of the Civil War, he addressed loyal Unionists with his firm sentiments in "The Death of Lincoln" and "The Death of Slavery."

As rallying points for public opinion, the poems about Lincoln and about slavery are models of their kind. The first stanza of the elegy captures the indelible force of Lincoln's personality and combines neatly his antithetical virtues of strength and compassion:

> Oh, slow to smite and swift to spare,
> Gentle and merciful and just!
> Who in the fear of God, didst bear
> The sword of power, a nation's trust![25]

"The Death of Slavery" skillfully, if extravagantly, mobilizes Gothic terror, religious piety, nationalistic fervor, and moralistic sentiment in denouncing involuntary servitude. It is the voice of the publicist who not only sought out the bias of his audience but strove to direct it to his purposes. In sanctifying the martyred leader of the Union cause, Bryant also kept his eye on Lincoln's benevolent policies for reconstruction. In celebrating the demise of Negro slavery, Bryant condemned the cowards and hypocrites who had defended it and were still potential enemies of freedom.

These poems, except of course the fantasies, are motivated by the activism of "The Antiquity of Freedom." Similarly, "Italy" (1860) praises the courage and determination of the rebellious populace, and "A Brighter Day" (1867), while lamenting the triumph of revolutionary forces, looks forward to the eventual liberation of the Spanish people. Poetry becomes, even more than it had in "The Ages" and "The Conjunction of Venus and Jupiter," a vehicle for propaganda. The ideas that had once been probed and resolved have become tempered into a steel blade for use in the political battles of the era.

If the questing poet in William Cullen Bryant had withered away in the glare of public life, the informed and eager partisan still remained, willing to dedicate his energies and talent, if not to the search for truth, at least to the maintenance of a society in which truth could flourish.

Chapter Five
"To Wander Forth"

William Cullen Bryant's reputation as an American man of letters has rested largely on his poetic rendering of native themes and subject matter. His embrace of the American landscape, his frequent allusions to American flora and fauna, his praise of American historical events and their heroes, and his dedication to national ideals have long merited this recognition. But, like many others of his generation—Irving, Cooper, and Longfellow in particular—he strove toward a more cosmopolitan vision. As I have noted, his politics embraced aspirations for liberty that were far more than a parochial Americanism, extending, as they did, to many other lands. And this was not merely an abstract idealism, for at the time of his migration to New York City in the 1820s he was already developing his facility in modern languages and reading widely in other languages. When in the next decade his responsibilities for the management of his newspaper could be delegated to William Leggett, he began a lifetime of frequent travel and residency abroad.

Bryant's aspirations toward broader horizons were never a denial of his Americanism; the expatriate route of Henry James, which so many writers would follow, was never part of his makeup. He acquired few if any affectations from his reading and travels—if one ignores the beard grown during his foray into the Near East in the 1850s—but rather absorbed his new knowledge and understanding into an essentially American point of view. While no innocent abroad, as Mark Twain ironically viewed himself, Bryant judged his experiences in Europe, the Near East, and Latin America largely in terms derived from his own provincial New England background—with seriousness, a penchant for moralizing, and pervasive intellectualism. He was not excessively judgmental of other modes of life, but instead tempered his negative reactions with prudence and common sense. His sympathies were, of course, with the common people, the joys and tragedies of their everyday lives, their unthinking piety and their efforts to survive through hard labor.

He appears to have recognized a higher impetus toward his reaching out beyond his native shores. While he never seems to describe himself in terms of a universal wanderlust, his poem "On the Death of Schiller" reveals something beneath the calm and somber surface that was more than Yankee inquisitiveness:

> 'Tis said, when Schiller's death drew nigh,
>   The wish possessed his mighty mind,
> To wander forth wherever lie
>   The homes and haunts of humankind.
>
> Then strayed the poet, in his dreams,
>   By Rome and Egypt's ancient graves;
> Went up the New World's forest-streams,
>   Stood in the Hindoo's temple-caves;
>
> Walked with the Pawnee, fierce and stark,
>   The sallow Tartar, midst his herds,
> The peering Chinese, and the dark
>   False Malay, uttering gentle words.
>
> How could he rest? even then he trod
>   The threshold of the world unknown;
> Already from the seat of God,
>   A ray upon his garments shone;—
>
> Shone and awoke the strong desire
>   For love and knowledge reached not here,
> Till, freed by death, his soul on fire
>   Sprang to a fairer, ampler sphere.[1]

The *Letters*

Although Bryant attributed the desire to wander to Schiller, it was no less his own, motivating his frequent journeys and resulting in a substantial body of writing, primarily travel sketches he composed both in the United States and abroad for publication as *Letters* in the *Evening Post*. The content of these dispatches, miscellaneous as it was, has been described in chapter 1. The *Letters* are informative enough, as far as they go, with descriptions of scenery and interesting sites, discussions of art and politics, and vignettes of the daily life of the people. The style, while sometimes less than polished, is lucid and accessible, with scattered moments of eloquence. There are entertaining passages and some knowledgeable insights into the people and places along the way.

Bryant's strength lie in his capacity to contemplate, to put himself in touch with the universality of nature, and to compress his ideas and feelings into telling metaphors. His letters generally lack what a Hawthorne or an Irving could give of the sense of place, and that momentary involvement of the reader that is the essence of narrative art, whether in fiction or the retelling of actual experiences. It follows that his travel writing lacks the immediacy of personal involvement—the narrator as romantic hero in his adventures abroad—that one finds in the writings of travel by Bayard Taylor or the widely read and discussed book of the time by Richard Henry Dana, Jr., *Two Years before the Mast* (1840), for which Bryant had been instrumental in securing publication.

Having said this for the pervasive character of the *Letters,* there are still some noteworthy passages. There is, for example, his description of the view from his lodgings in Florence on his first visit to Italy. Thomas Cole had painted a similar view, and, as Bryant was to describe in a private letter, he was sensitive to and appreciative of the way in which the Italian light, so appealing to American painters of the era, enhanced the scene:

To the north and west, the peaks of the Apennines are in full sight, rising over the spires of the city and the groves of the Cascine. Every evening I see them through the soft, delicately-colored haze of an Italian sunset, looking as if they had caught something of the transparency of the sky, and appearing like mountains of fairy-land, instead of the bleak and barren ridges of rock which they really are.[2]

He was to incorporate this vision into his poem, "To the Apennines" (1835), finding in the "fairy-land" imagery a symbol for the political aspirations of the Italian nationalists.

There is the short passage in which he recounts his emotions on the upper Nile where the antiquity and vastness of the temple of Karnac took possession of him:

As I sat among the forest of gigantic columns in the great court of the temple of Karnac, it appeared to me that after such a sight no building reared by human hands could affect me with a sense of sublimity. Seen through the vista of columns to the east was a small grove of palms close to the ruins, and another to the west; their tall and massive trunks looked slender and low, compared to the enormous shafts of stone around me. I looked up to where the clouds, floating slowly over, seemed almost to touch them with their skirts, and perceived that two or three of them, shaken perhaps by an earthquake from their upright position, stood leaning against their fellows, still upon bearing upon their capitals portions of the enormous architrave which belonged to them. Thus they have stood, and thus they doubtless will stand for ages; scarce anything, but another earthquake can bring them to the ground.[3]

This is a unique statement for Bryant. The "sublime" for him, as for most American literary figures, was to be found exclusively in nature, and to have found the temple at Karnac, a human monument, to have affected him with "the sense of sublimity" was a radical departure from the norms of his sensibility.

Quite different, but equally intense, were his reactions upon visiting the tomb of Napoleon Bonaparte during his visit to Paris in 1853. He is moved to capture the irony of the occasion, a rare instance of this in his writing, but the moralistic reflection with which the passage closes is quite typical:

Passing beside the glittering altar, we descended a flight of steps to the level of the great Court of the *Invalides*. . . . On each side of this passage to the sarcophagus stands a colossal figure, in bronze; one of them bearing, on a cushion, a globe and sceptre, the symbols of dominion, and the other a sword and gauntlet, emblematic of the violence by which that dominion was gained, and, for a brief space, upheld. As we were considering these figures, the voices of priests and a choir, chanting at the altar above, resounded up the lofty dome: it was a litany, nominally addressed to the God of Peace. I looked about me, and saw only the symbols of warlike glory, and encouragement to the pursuit of renown in arms. . . . This church itself had been converted into the mausoleum of a conqueror; it was the shrine of Napoleon; this altar formed a part of his monument, and this hymn, whatever its words, was chanted in his honor. I had before me one of the forms in which the Power of Destruction is still worshipped. . . . I left it with the strong impression of the yet imperfect civilization of mankind.[4]

The entire account from which this passage has been excerpted reveals the New England background of William Cullen Bryant: his adversion to military glory, his suspicion of pomp and ceremony, particularly when used to palliate the dynamics of imperialism, and his intellectual resistance to the emotionally charged experience.

Not that all of his experiences were so exalting, or his encounters with death so dignified. In Paris he had visited *La Morgue,* where the bodies fished from the Seine were put on public display so that they might be claimed by relatives. And after capturing his vivid impressions of the cemetery of Pere la Chaise, he moralized upon the burial place of the poor,

. . . where those who have dwelt apart from their more fortunate fellow-creatures in life lie apart in death. Here are no walks, no shade of trees, no planted shrubbery, but ridges of raw earth, and tufts of course herbage show where the bodies are thrown together under a thin covering of soil. I was about to walk over the spot, but was repelled by the sickening exhalations that rose from it.[5]

The poverty of European peasants and slum dwellers is often described in his *Letters,* anticipating the American realists and naturalists of the late nineteenth century. While Bryant the traveler tries to maintain his surface neutrality in such passages, his distress is apparent enough. In a letter from Scotland he turns from an enthusiastic description of the architectural and scenic beauty of Edinburgh to the conditions of the impoverished:

From this magnificence of nature and art, the transition was painful to what I saw of the poorer population. . . . Hither a throng of sickly-looking, dirty people, bringing with them their unhealthy children, had crawled from the narrow wynds or alleys on each side of the street. We entered several of these wynds, and passed down one of them, between houses of vast height, story piled upon story, till we came to the deep hollow of the Cowgate. Children were swarming in the way, all of them, bred in that close and impure atmosphere, of a sickly appearance, and the aspect of premature age in some of them, which were carried in arms, was absolutely frightful.[6]

Bryant's characterizations of individuals met in his travels is, in the main, perfunctory, merely a supporting piece of detail for the event he is relating at the time. A few memorable sketches of picturesque personalities may be discovered, though, such as those of the deranged gentleman called "Cheswick" in the Lunatic Society in Hanwell, near London; the plump, young Arab woman in Oran with her gay costume and heavy facial makeup; or the conversational botanist, Mr. Fortune, met aboard a ship crossing the Mediterranean. The most colorful, however, was Emanuel Balthus, who led the caravan in which Bryant and his companions traveled camel-back across the Arabian Desert to Jerusalem:

At our head, armed with a long sabre and carrying a rifle, rode Emanuel Balthus, our dragoman, an Athenian by birth, speaking the ancient Greek as well as the Romaic, fluent in Italian, Turkish and Arabic, intelligible in French, and in a fair way to learn English. . . . [He had] the manners of a nobleman, active, prompt, anxious to satisfy his employers, as choleric and as generous as a prince, a little too much given to flogging his Arabs, but always attaching them to him by the liberality with which he treats them.[7]

For the most part the *Letters* are unencumbered by narrative art beyond the straightforward account of places visited, anecdotes, snatches of conversation, and, of course, description. The letters in which Bryant sustains a short narrative, in spite of his reportorial style, stand out. His passage through the Tyrol in 1835, at times in a heavy snow storm, comes to life. His witnessing of a religious procession, his encounter with the innkeeper who refused to serve him meat on a religious holiday, and the appearance at the inn of a group of travelers "who poured forth their orisons in the German language for half an hour with no small appearance of fervency," all combine to make an engaging sketch.[8]

In 1853, on his way into Syria, Bryant and his companions, in addition to a number of other travelers, were compelled to undergo five days of quarantine at Gaza, three of the days in a walled enclosure called a *lazaretto*. The incarceration itself they accepted with equanimity, but they faced the problem of how to spend their time. They read, wrote, and paced by the wall; they looked at the surrounding country and nearby town, over which swept "the shadows of clouds brought by a cool wind from the sea"; they observed the women washing clothes and watched "our friends, the dervishes [holy men] and pilgrims, at their devotions, prostrating themselves from time to time, in their prayers, which they uttered inaudibly, with moving lips." When these five dervishes were not praying, Bryant noted, they either slept in the sun or picked the lice from their garments. The sketch also includes the encounter between the dervishes and a pet monkey that "tore their rags and sacred skins without mercy," and the shrill antics of an Arab woman quarreling with one of the innkeepers. A short interview with a French physician, in which they accede to his request that they all stick out their tongues, and he declares them fit, concludes the sketch.[9] It has a Hemingway feel to it—the language is more terse than usual for Bryant, the observations incisive, the subject matter exotic at first but becoming flatly prosaic in the development. The tone of the whole approaches that ominous quality of many of the stories of *In Our Time*.

Considering the background of both Hemingway and Bryant in American journalism, it is not too surprising that they shared an interest in exact, verifiable detail and in the suppression of editorial comment; both were aware of how fugitive the interest of newspaper readers could be. Thus, Bryant's description of the bullfight he attended during his trip to Spain in 1857 is little more than a thousand words, but it is crammed with sharp visual images, which, for the most part, are presented in prose devoid of explicit commentary. As this excerpt illustrates, the event itself conveys its own emotional impact:

Finally the people began to call for the dogs. *Los perros! los perros!* rose from a thousand throats. Three large dogs were brought, which, barking loudly, flew at the bull with great fury. He took them one by one on his horns, and threw them up in the air; one of them he caught on his fall, and tossed him again. The dogs tore his ears into strings, but they were soon either disabled or cowed, and only attacked him warily, while he kept them off by presenting them first one horn and then the other.[10]

Bryant does not completely avoid interjecting his feelings. At one point, the horse of a *picador* is gored by the bull, his bowels ripped open. Bryant comments, "I then perceived, with a sort of horror, that the horse had been blindfolded, in order that he might not get out of the way of the bull." And he concludes, after the dispatching of the second bull, in a way that presumably would have disgusted Hemingway, "I had now seen enough, and left the place amidst the thunders of applause which the creature's fall drew from the crowd." To give him credit, however, he did not include in his *Letter* the comment that appears in his diary, "We went to the cathedral to compose ourselves."[11]

The *Letters*, then, while hardly exemplary of the genre of travel literature, show us a writer whose talents radiated in many directions. It further demonstrates that Bryant was no reclusive poetic soul but a man with the confidence and determination to meet head on the ways of foreign lands. It is the very nature of wanderlust to be insatiable, and Bryant continued his excursions into his later years. He was in his seventies when he took his final long and arduous sea voyage to Europe.

The Translator

In his personal quest for a broader, more universal culture, Bryant read widely literatures in other languages and passed on to his readers the results of these encounters through selective translations of poetry. While the amount of his translation from the modern languages was not as extensive as say, that of Henry Wadsworth Longfellow, and he was more popularizer than scholar, the translations are a noteworthy part of his literary work. Only in his later years, when he undertook the translation of Homer's epics, did he fully devote himself to the task, making an even further contribution to widening of the horizons of the American reading public.

He was well aware of the limitations and difficulties of translating poetry from one language to another. Every translator has to choose which is more important, to convey the sense and spirit of the original or strive for a literal equivalency. Must the meter and rhyme scheme of the original be preserved, even at the expense of fluid expression? Or should the poet–translator impose upon the verses a cadence more natural to his own language? Should the translator take liberties with imagery and metaphors that may be conventional in the foreign verse but unrecognizable to readers in his own language?

To these problems Bryant brought his practical good sense. He was scrupulous, attentive to the meanings of the words in their context, and alert to the interplay of rhythm and content. Some of his lines are close to literal translations, others have been modified for the sake of the poem and its comprehension by the reader. For instance, many of his translations have subtitles or notes stating "From the Spanish," or when he wished to designate the original poet, "From the German of Uhland." In a note to his English version of La Fontaine's "L'amour et la Folie," he even admitted, "This is rather an imitation than a translation of the poem of the graceful fabulist."[12] Bryant had, indeed, lengthened the poem by nine lines, subjected La Fontaine' scansion and rhymes to a regularity more congenial to his audience, and softened the touches of irony, which, to the American ear would have seemed both frivolous and cynical.

Bryant's "The Hurricane" was followed by a note of explanation that this poem was "nearly a translation" of one by Jose Maria de Heredia. [13] (Bryant omitted the last eleven lines, presumably because of their blatant religiosity.)

Bryant would seldom drastically alter the stanza scheme of the original, but he once pointed out that the rhymes in other languages are more easily found than in English. Thus he would sometimes rhyme alternate lines of a quatrain instead of completing them all. He adhered closely, however, to the sense of the whole. While the precise ideas and tonal values might, to the scholarly ear, be somewhat less accurate, subtle, or finely tuned than desirable, the poetry makes up in readability what it may lack in sophistication.

For the most part, in selecting poems for translation, Bryant stayed close to his own proclivities in subject matter—ballads and sentimental love lyrics and poems about nature. Usually he translated only a single work by any one poet, but there were a few exceptions, notably two by the German poet Uhland, two by the Cuban, Heredia, the collection of short *Fabula* by Rosas, and both of Homer's epics. He seems to have been motivated by universality rather than by specialization, and, of course, this was in keeping with his role as a transmitter of foreign culture to American society.

His youthful schooling, much of it spent in the traditional busywork of translating the classics, stood him in good stead when he acquired his skills in French, Spanish, and German. He learned French and Spanish during the 1820s, soon after arriving in New York City. He immediately began translating and wrote critical essays on medieval poetry for the *Talisman*—the troubadours of southern France and the so-called Morescan Romances of Spain. An extended stay in Germany in 1835 promoted his competency in that country's language, and most of his translations from the German are from that period.

For the *Talisman*, Bryant reviewed a book that had been reissued in France, *The Lives of the Troubadours,* by a sixteenth-century writer, John of Nostradamus, and in a second essay, drawing upon this work, he tells of a competition before the court between the poetry of Pierre Vidal and that of Bernard Rascas. [14] Bryant translated their poems from the *langue d'oc,* as part of the essay. Vidal's lyric, "Love in the Age of Chivalry," was, Bryant told his readers, applauded by the court for breaking away from classical images in his personification of Love and "had clothed it in new and striking forms and allusions, borrowed directly from the age of chivalry in which he lived." Bernard Rascas had met the challenge with a poem, "The Love of God," which was judged superior "Inasmuch as the love of God was nobler than the love of woman, and the verses of Bernard Rascas were of nobler invention than the verses of Pierre Vidal."

Of the two poems, Vidal's was the lighter and more lyrical, as befitting his theme of earthly love. Bryant captures effectively the lilt of the short iambic lines and rhymed quatrains. Bernard Rascas's "The Love of God," because of its compressed imagery, was wisely elected by Bryant to be translated into a sextameter line, which produced an even more dirgelike effect than the original. To the writer of "Thanatopsis," this may have seemed quite appropriate. The final lines bear his mark as well as that of Bernard Rascas:

> And the great globe itself, so the holy writings
>   tell
> With the rolling firmament, where the starry
>   armies dwell,
> Shall melt with fervent heat—shall all pass away,
> Except the love of God, which
>   shall live and last for aye. [15]

In another essay for the *Talisman*, Bryant discussed the "Moriscan Romances" of fourteenth-century Spain, and again translated the illustrative poems. Their writers have been obscured by history, but, as Bryant tells in his essay, they were still part of the oral tradition of the Spanish people. Not having been to Spain at this time, he took some literary liberties in telling his readers, "To enjoy them as you ought, you should hear them sung by a Spanish maiden, under a Spanish sky . . . from the small windows of those *casas morunas,* as they are called—those solid dwellings built centuries ago by Moorish architects . . ."[16] Indeed, the Moriscan Romances, as their name implies, were composed by the Moors to celebrate the loves and the victories of the Knights of Grenada. But while this speaks to Bryant's enthusiasm for an ancient folk poetry, his translations hardly captured the charm of a song by a Spanish maiden under a Spanish sky.

He also translated Spanish poetry of subsequent periods, by Bartholomé Leonardo de Argensola and Luis Ponce de Léon (also known as Fray Luis de Léon) of the sixteenth century, by Estaban Manuel de Villegas, Castro y Añaya, and Francisco de Rioja of the seventeenth, and José de la Casaban Iglesias of the eighteenth century. These are predominantly lyrics of nature, the notable exception being Argensola's "Mary Magdalen," which tells of Christ's forgiveness for the fallen woman (Bryant's only treatment of defiled womanhood in his collected works).

Bryant's translation of "The Rivulet" by Castro y Añaya is an interesting instance of his finding congenial topics. He had long been attracted to the symbolic possibilities of rivers and streams, having previously composed his own poem "The Rivulet" (1824). Añaya's poem, like Bryant's, dealt with the themes of youth and age as they were suggested by the ever-flowing water.

From a critical standpoint, however, the most successful of these translations is "Song" by José de la Casaban Iglesias, a poet–priest of the Salamancan School. Iglesias wittily transposes the conventional lament of the male lover, who would ritualistically bemoan the unresponsiveness of his fair lady, to the perspective of the woman. This lady expresses her dismay at being the victim of propriety:

> Alexis calls me cruel:
>   The rifted crags that hold
> The gathered ice of winter,
>   He says, are not more cold.
>
> When even the very blossoms
>   Around the fountain's brim,
> And forest walks, can witness
>   The love I bear to him.
>
> I would that I could utter
>   My feelings without shame,
> And tell him how I love him,
>   Nor wrong my virgin fame.
>
> Alas! to seize the moment
>   When heart inclines to heart,
> And press a suit with passion,
>   Is not a woman's part.
>
> If man come not to gather
>   The roses where they stand,

> They fade among the foliage;
> They cannot seek his hand. [17]

In translating "Song," Bryant has respected the simplicity and
the lyric strength of the original and yet made it available to the
contemporary sensibility. One might fault his reaching for the forced
rhymes of brim—him and shame—fame, but, as he points out, the
rhymes in Spanish are much easier to come by than they are in
English. And from the point of view of the reader of the New York
Mirror, neither rhyme would have been disruptive to the tone or
meaning of the poem.

Toward Spanish poetry of his own time he was equally receptive.
His association with Carolina Coronado de Perry, the wife of the
American legate to the Spanish court when Bryant visited there in
1857, is documented in his note to his translation of her "El pájaro
perdido" ("The Lost Bird"). The verse, thirty lines of affected grief
over a pet bird that has flown his coop, was, one would hope,
translated simply as a courtesy toward the attractive and passionate
Mrs. Perry. In addition to *The Hurricane* (1828) by Heredia, Bryant
collaborated on a translation of the Cuban poet's *Niágra,* which
Bryant believed to be "the best that has been written about the
great American cataract."[18] Collected in the posthumous edition of
Bryant's poetry are the translations of a series of "Fables" in verse,
attributed to a Mexican poet, José Rosas. They are in the vein of
La Fontaine, witty and with moralistic messages that were, no
doubt, appealing to Bryant.

The earliest of Bryant's translations from the German to appear
in print was a ballad, "The Count of Griers" (1836) by his contemporary Johann Ludwig Uhland. Much of Uhland's work derived
from folk legends and themes, celebrating the German national
past. Perhaps Longfellow had brought Uhland to Bryant's attention
during their frequent visits in Heidelberg, where Bryant stayed for
six weeks in 1835–36, for Longfellow also made translations of
Uhland's *Dichtung.* Bryant would later translate a second poem by
Uhland, *"Das Lied vom Mägdlein und dem Ringe,"* which appeared in
Graham's Magazine in 1843 as "A Northern Legend."

In *"Der Graf von Greirs"* Bryant had good material in work with:
a romantic tale of a nobleman's attempt to revert to a simpler,
carefree life and his eventual restoration to his life of responsibility. [19]
It tells of the Count, lord of the manor, who becomes enthralled

by the festive singing and dancing of wandering herdsmen and maidens, among them one especially fair maiden. He leaves to revel with them in their mountain hideaway. A violent storm arises and he is caught in a torrent that spares his companions. The flood waters carry him down the mountain and, with doleful pangs of sorrow, he returns to his grim castle.

Not only does Uhland's poem convey the lure of the innocent and primitive so characteristic of German romanticism, but it is alive with imagery of the mountains, the costumes, and the fury of the storm, all of which were congenial to Bryant's taste. His handling of the poetics is subtle and effective. He maintains Uhland's structure of the poem, ten modified Nibelungen stanzas (two pair of rhymed lines), although he allowed himself to transpose phrases of the original between adjacent lines. While he stays close to the literal translation, he maintains the poetic quality. In describing the dancing peasants, Bryant picks up Uhland's *"Die weissen Ärmel schimmern"* and renders it capably with "the white sleeves flit and glimmer." Uhland's imagery of *"bunt slattern Band and Kranz"* he even improves upon with "the wreathes and ribbons toss." He is marginally less successful in describing the storm. For *"Geborsten ist die Wolfe, der Bach zum Strom geschwellt,"* Bryant falls somewhat short with "The cloud has shed its waters, the brook comes swollen down." It is regrettable that he cushions the final line of the poem in both the imagery and its harsh consonance: *"Nimm mich in dein Mauren, du ödes Grafenhaus"* is translated as "And thou, my cheerless mansion, receive thy master back." But the narrative of this exotic and sentimental tale is transposed into English in a coherent and convincing fashion, quite in tune with the nineteenth-century American sensibility. Bryant also translated another ballad, "The Lady of the Castle of Warwick" by Adelbert de Chamisso, a fashionable poet of the early nineteenth century and a member of the literary circle of Madame de Staël.

An even greater challenge for Bryant as a translator was Goethe's love lyric, "Nähe Des Geliebten," literally translated as "Near to the Loved One." Bryant took the opening phrase *"Ich denke dein"*— "I Think of Thee" for the title of his poem, which he published in *Godey's Lady's Book* in 1844. Considering that Bryant stayed very close to the Goethe's imagery and respected the complex structure of the original quatrains—not only the a b a b rhyme but the alternation of full six-stress lines with half-lines—he does remarkably well:

> I think of thee when the strong rays of noon
> Flash from the sea;
> When the clear fountains glimmer in the moon,
> I think of thee.
>
> I see thee when along the distant way
> The dust-clouds creep,
> And in the night, when trembling travelers stray
> By chasm and steep.
>
> I hear thee when the tides go murmuring soft
> To the calm air;
> In lone and stilly woods I listen oft,
> And hear thee there.
>
> I am with thee—I know thee from afar,
> Yet dream thee near;
> The sun goes down; star brightens after star;
> Would thou wert here![20]

The lover's cry from the heart was not Bryant's usual voice, and Goethe's lyric depends very much upon the rhythm and nuances of meaning in the German tongue, but it is a credit to Bryant's technical facility that the translation reads as well as it does. He is forced to rely too heavily on a poetic vocabulary as in "chasm and steep," "oft," "art," and "wert," Such diction was, of course, his practice in his own verse, but it is too stilted to convey the plain and intimate expression of Goethe's poem.

Other translations from the German were of a quite different sort. An anonymous poem "The Sharpening of the Sabre" (1836) conveys the lusty enthusiasm of a warrior preparing for one more struggle. "The Paradise of Tears" (1843), by a little-known poet, Niclas Müller, picks up the themes of innocence and death in Nature, so congenial to Bryant. "The Words of the Koran" (1865), from a poem by Joseph Christian von Zedlitz, is a moral lesson set within an oriental fable. "The Poet's First Song" (1876), from Ernst Christoph Houwald, is a sentimental reminiscence by a poet who hears his early melody sung by a sweetheart of his early days.

But most unusual in its irony and surreal quality is "The Saw Mill" (1850). Translated from *"Der Wandrer in der Sägemühle"* of Justinus Kerner, it tells of a "wanderer," who, passing by a saw mill, hears the voice of a tree crying that the "cruel engine / Is passing through my heart."[21] And then he hears, with a shudder, the prophecy that the planks that fall from the blade are those of his own casket: "This wood shall form the chamber / Whose walls shall close thee in." This dark fantasy ends on a note of pathetic irony: "Then, as I tried to answer, / At once the wheel was still." Bryant retains much of the rhyme scheme and cadence of the original as well as its simplicity. Kerner's poem may have been more skillfully wrought, having several contrived shifts of tonal effects, but Bryant's translation conveys well enough the irony and the horror of the brief narrative.

As a translator, Bryant had his limitations, but on the whole he was surprisingly effective. He brought before the English-speaking public a wide variety of works in several modern languages (there are also single poems in Italian and Portugese) and, as this brief survey has pointed out, numerous styles and a range of topics. He respected the formal structures of the poems and departed from them only in the interests of clarity. Some of the translations are creditable in their own right, without reference to their originals, or to their historical contexts. They are invariably accessible to the literate reader, and while they served to popularize literature in foreign tongues, they also show evidences of a scholarly concern for accuracy.

In 1863, during the trying days of the Civil War, Bryant began his translation of the Homeric epics. His biographer quotes him as saying, "I was only trying my hand on the Greek to see how much of it I retained."[22] The task took on greater import for him, however, as he surveyed the current translations, and in 1867 he was to write to a friend that "It was an experiment on my part, and I have been curious to know how it appears to those who read it. It differs from all others in English by its greater simplicity."[23] He was proud that his translations of the *Odyssey* and *Iliad,* while retaining the qualities of Homer's poetry, were also more accurate in their rendering of the ancient Greek than the other versions being read in his day, notably those of William Cooper (1791) and Lord Derby (1864).

As Thomas G. Voss has pointed out, Bryant's decision to adapt the poems to blank verse, instead of the hexameters of the original, was based upon his desire to keep the language natural. In his preface to the *Iliad* Bryant stated that blank verse "enabled me to keep more closely to the original in my rendering, without any sacrifice of ease or of spirit of expression."[24] He also explained that he retained the formulaic epithets, "making Achilles swift-footed and Ulysses fertile in resources." According to Voss, it was the combination of the pentameter line and the retention of the epithets that resulted in a translation that was twenty-five percent longer than the original.

Bryant's claims as to the fidelity of his translation should, however, be kept in perspective. He was troubled by the ancient Greek gods, whom, he wrote his brother, behaved "shamefully" and were "detestable." Thus, his version tends to moderate their behavior.[25] As for Ulysses and his lapse from Victorian standards of sexual morality during his sojourn with the nymph, Calypso, Bryant glosses over the more explicit passages in order to make them minimally offensive to his readers. For example, where Robert Fitzgerald tells us that Odysseus and Calypso "retired, this pair, to the inner cave / To revel and rest softly side by side," and where Richmond Lattimore translates the Greek as "[they] enjoyed themselves in love and stayed all night by each other," Bryant would have them "side by side, / They took their rest."[26]

The seven years spent by Bryant on the translations were well rewarded by a favorable critical reception and healthy sales. As contributions to the enlightenment of American culture, these works are too often overlooked, as are Bryant's translations from the modern languages. They all serve to remind us of the ways in which a poet can, by freeing himself of the restraints of provincialism, promote the advancement of not only literary culture, but the more general culture as well.

Chapter Six
The Divided Voice

If Bryant's vacillation between epideictic and contemplative verse in his poems of progress was, on one level, a re-enactment of the age-old dilemma of the personal poet who feels compelled to tithe his talent to the social good, on a more profound level this indecision was too symptomatic of the fundamental weakness of his poetry. Bryant was seldom able to speak with the firm, clear, original voice of his own genius. Though he sensed early and rightly that his was the way of the poet, he never truly understood the terms of his vocation. Though his voice in a few great poems rises to uniqueness, the grounds for his triumphs were never clear to him. And though at times he brought into the realm of the articulate his personal vision of the universal experience, he seemed unable to sustain his best insights and to profit by his successes.

This basic criticism of Bryant as a poet need not obscure, however, our appreciation of his many accomplishments. Bryant—given his nature and environment—faced an inevitable and nearly unsolvable dilemma. His preternaturally early development, his search for parental approval, the facile action of his mind as it worked backward and forward between experience and introspection, the unquestioned authority of British culture, the fluid state of American letters, and criticism during the years of his maturation—all of these militated against the kind of ultimate commitment required of the creative artist. Out of his dilemma he made the best that might have been anticipated. He dignified nature both as a subject and as a metaphor, he made some of his deeper thoughts available to the masses, he not only expressed himself in the discipline of traditional meters but also pioneered in the use of freer, more natural rhythms.

Yet Bryant could never make the basic decision that Emerson was to formulate as the choice between self-reliance and conformity. To have fallen back upon his own resources would have meant isolation and obscurity; to have molded himself deliberately on the pattern of an acknowledged poet—Wordsworth or Byron—would have meant the sacrifice of his independence as a Yankee and an

American. Either choice would have guaranteed his work a fullness and consistency; either choice would have allowed him to mine his talent more deeply and to understand the dynamics of his creative process. But the choice was not made. His poetic gift broadened—to use Emerson's figure—in concentric circles and not according to any linear directive. As a poet he was an eclectic, as an individual, a pragmatist. Unlike the great modern poets—Yeats, Rilke, Eliot, Stevens—who would build in part upon the failures of their predecessors, Bryant faced the problems of multiplicity and divided purpose with a gift for adaptability rather than with integrity and self-awareness. Lacking within him the tight knot of conviction, he could never fulfill the promise implicit in his vocation.

This pathetic flaw influenced every aspect of his poetry, but it is most noticeable in the two areas with which this chapter will deal: poetic theory and poetic technique. In his infrequent attempts to reflect upon his art, Bryant was never able to formulate an adequate conception of the relationship between poetic ends and poetic means. If he resisted the mechanical functionalism of the classical rhetoric he had absorbed through his formal education, he also balked at the obvious alternative—a thoroughgoing aestheticism. Neither "art for morality's sake" nor "art for art's sake" provided him with a rationale for his own creativity. Thus, his critical fumblings expose only too well his policy of drifting between the neoclassical Scylla and the romantic Charybdis.

Poetic Theory

His sole effort at sustained criticism, The *Lectures on Poetry* (1825–26), manfully attempted to declare a position on this issue of ends and means. In the second of the four lectures, entitled "On the Value and Uses of Poetry," he defined the ultimate end of poetry as moral uplift and spiritual refinement. While admitting that a good deal of poetry is mere "amusement, an agreeable intellectual exercise," Bryant stressed the nobler goals: "[Poetry] has, however, a still higher value when regarded as in some sort the support of our innocence, for there is ever something pure and elevated in the creations of poetry. Its spirit is an aspiration after superhuman beauty and majesty, which, if it has no affinity with, has at least some likeness to virtue."[1]

How are these goals to be reached? Three positive recommen-

dations may be gleaned from the *Lectures:* first, American poetry
should tap the rich resources of native speech and natural imagery;
second, poetry should profit from the poetic "experiments" of the
past rather than strive for novelty; third, poetry should be "suggestive" and not attempt literal representation. Independently, each of
these methods could produce an aesthetic experience that might be
considered ennobling and spiritual. The first—that of tapping native
resources—is, indeed, the way that Whitman chose; the second is
that of the traditionalist Longfellow; the third approximates the
path of mysterious ambiguity by which Poe climbed toward the
"supernal." But, in combination, the methods are unstable and too
often ineffective. Like the man who believed in all religions in hopes
of hitting upon one that was right, Bryant, in his criticism as well
as in his poetry, obscured his purpose through the multiplicity of
his means. While there is nothing intrinsically wrong about using
traditional verse forms to praise American scenery, as Bryant did
repeatedly, the total effect of the poem is as much conditioned by
the imported stanzaic patterns as it is by the vastness and wildness
of the landscape. And in similar fashion the total effect of the poem
derives as much from the "suggestive" manner in which the scene
is described as it does upon the natural details of physical location.
Thus, what Bryant conceived as various roads to the same city were
actually variable determinants that could shift the locus of the des-
tination across the surface of a map. Bryant failed to see that the
poetic end was absolutely dependent upon the poetic means—that
a diversity of means did not simplify but, to the contrary, complicated the creative process.

Particularly in his treatment of the idea of "suggestion" does his
theorizing expose his confusion. For Bryant, the "suggestive" power
of poetry arose from its capacity to encourage the imagination along
"the path which the poet only points out, and shapes its visions
from the scenes and allusions which he gives." As a "suggestive
art" poetry stands in contrast to the "imitative" arts of painting and
sculpture, which only reproduce "sensible objects." While these
"imitative" arts carefully define reality in its form and substance,
poetry utilizes "arbitrary symbols" (language) in order to excite the
imagination "most powerfully and delightfully." To Bryant, examples of great poetry that affect the imagination are Milton's por-
trayals of Eve and Satan.[2] In each case the imagination feeds upon
a few hints in order to visualize the physical and moral qualities of

the character. Had Bryant been satisfied to expand upon this point, his conception of poetry would have been unified and usable—perhaps even comparable to that put forward by Poe in "The Poetic Principle." But, still suspicious of the currents of unregulated "imagination," he foundered upon the shoals of common sense.

From the point at which Bryant took up in his essay the roles of *emotion* and *intellect* in poetry, the idea of "suggestion" is all but forgotten. Once the door has been opened to "the language of the passions" and to "direct lessons of wisdom," then the sources of imaginative vitality—mystery, wonder, spontaneity—retire to their private chambers. Once the "suggestive" power of poetry becomes comprehensive enough to include the familiar rhetorical devices for kindling emotions and instilling ideas, there is little left in poetry to distinguish it from prose. In fact, such is the conclusion at which Bryant, at the close of his first *Lecture,* sadly and quietly arrives. He admits that the only way in which he can distinguish between poetry and "eloquence" is by metrical arrangement.[3] This conclusion, far removed from the brave premise upon which he had built his critical remarks, is a clear indication of his inability to maintain a consistent understanding of his creative work.

Form and Diction

In Bryant's attitude toward poetic form, as in his theories of poetry, there is a fundamental deficiency. Even a rapid perusal of the collected poetry reveals his constant experimentation with rhyme schemes, stanzaic units, and meter. Although much of his verse is in rhymed quatrains, he adapted easily to the sonnet form, the Spenserian measure, and the ballad. He was adept at both conventional rhyme schemes and improvised patterns. In "To a Waterfowl," for example, he skillfully combines trimeters and pentameters within the rhymed quatrain. "Green River" is a marvelous use of rhymed tetrameter couplets to create a variety of effects. And in a number of poems, "Catterskill Falls" for one, he affixes this rhymed tetrameter couplet as a braking device at the conclusion of each conventional stanza.[4] Perhaps Bryant can be praised, as Professor McDowell has praised him, for the estimable virtues of versatility and liberality in his use of poetic form. But for the poet such praise is, at best, a kind of honorable mention. With each successive mastery of a form Bryant reaffirms his technical competence but seldom does the novel device stimulate discoveries of fresh ideas or emotions. Too often the experiment suggests that the poet is still straining for the better vehicle, still seeking for the external order of discipline that will bring his work to life. Instead of pressing the more viable forms to the limit of their capacity, he dissipates his strength upon a variety of minor problems. That very breadth and restlessness that characterized Bryant as a student of nature and society and makes him interesting as a journalist and traveler tended to produce a body of verse with more amplitude than depth, more intelligence than conviction.

Bryant appears not to have come to grips with the problem of language. His critical observations usually revolved around two key points. The first is obviously indebted to the viewpoint of Wordsworth, expressed in the preface to *The Lyrical Ballads,* in its appeal for a less stylized and more natural diction in poetry. Thus the poet—by omitting "stiff Latinisms," "hackneyed phrases," and "the recondite or remote allusion" from his verses—can acquire a "household" or "luminous" style.[5] Bryant praised the tendency of contemporary poets to go "directly to nature for their imagery, instead of taking it from what once had been regarded as the common stock of the guild of poets."[6]

The second point Bryant made about language in the *Lectures* was that the tongue spoken by Americans and available to the native poet was a successfully transplanted version of a basic Anglo–Saxon. Having the flexibility to meet the new political and scientific conditions of American life, this language still retained the beauty and integrity of its early roots. Bryant summarized his position thus: "It has grown up, as every forcible and beautiful language has done, among a simple and unlettered people; it has accommodated itself, in the first place, to the things of nature, and, as civilization advanced, to the things of art; and thus it has become a language full of picturesque forms of expression, yet fitted for the purposes of science."[7]

Both of these points were to become axiomatic for generations of American writers, not merely because they provided a rationalization for a national literature, but because their implications opened up new and exciting vistas for expression. The downright earthiness of the American vernacular, the latent ironies and humor of dialect, the possibilities of "organic" expression that united matter and idea in a single word or phrase—all of these were to announce those

great experiments in language by Whitman, Thoreau, Melville, and
Mark Twain. But Bryant failed to sense the implications of his
theory. For him the return to nature for diction meant merely the
naming of indigenous plants, birds, and animals in the simple
vernacular and the brief, infrequent mention of place names in his
poems. For Bryant the historical condition of the transplanted language implied none of the high ironies that ring through the rhetoric
of *Moby-Dick;* to the contrary, the diction of the poet should abhor
"subtleties of thought" and adhere "to the common track of human
intelligence."[8]

His confusion over the "suggestive" function of poetry spills over
into this area of diction. On the one hand, he explains in the *Lectures*
that language, for all its achievements, "is still limited and imperfect, and . . . falls infinitely short of the mighty and diversified
world of matter and thought of which it professes to be the representative."[9] And he conceives of the way in which descriptive
passages function as "glimpses of things thrown into the mind; here
and there a trace of an outline; here a gleam of light, and there a
dash of shade."[10] Yet, on the other hand, he could speak of language
as "a great machine"[11] and employ—as we have seen in his epideictic
verse—all of the mechanical devices for persuasion typical of util-
itarian rhetoric. Lacking any theoretical approach to language that
did any more than describe the current situation, Bryant was not
prepared to formulate an original position for his own work. His
poetic diction avoids the more obvious pedantry and artifice of earlier
American poets, which he had pointed out in some detail in an
essay-review of 1818;[12] yet he retained many vestiges of the former
style. And while the notion of "suggestion" brought an imaginative
vitality to his better poems, a workable concept was never to emerge
from the clouded background evoked by the *Lectures*.

Bryant sought no half-way house in prosody, as he had in poetic
diction. Instead, like Wordsworth and the Victorians, he stretched
his talent over both the traditional, melodic verse and the less
inhibited rhythms of blank verse. In both areas, as previous chapters
have illustrated, he had notable successes. Yet in neither area did
he develop, in theory or in practice, a prosody that could be relied
upon to sustain him through his creative adventures. Unlike a for-
malist such as Frost, Bryant did not find endless "the possibilities
for tune from the dramatic tones of meaning struck across the rigidity
of a limited meter."[13] Indeed, his "dramatic tones" have, through

the collected works, a discouraging similarity. Nor in blank verse did he always find the pitch and cadence that could keep pace with his intellectual and emotional discoveries. At times during his career—in "Thanatopsis," "The Fountain," and "The Antiquity of Freedom"—his poetic intent coincided with his choice of blank verse, and the promise of a forceful and original voice is made manifest. At other times, however, the long sequence of iambic pentameter lines (which are best read, as Northrop Frye points out, as a four-stress, running rhythm[14]), performed a pedestrian service, doing little to raise prose description and meditation to a level of poetic intensity.

The Formal Voice

Several examples of his formal voice at work can be found among Bryant's experiments in the sonnet form. No established poet in America had, previous to Bryant, been equal to the rigid demands of either the English or Italian variations of the form, and thus Bryant's achievements in this particular area take on a historical and artistic importance. Two sonnets composed in 1824, "Mutation" and "November," indicate the two directions opened up by the poet's concern for form; a third, "To Cole, the Painter, Departing for Europe," illustrates the level of achievement of which Bryant was capable had he persevered in his use of the sonnet.

In "Mutation" Bryant ambitiously adopted an interlocking rhyme scheme in which the fifth and eighth lines of the sonnet pick up the rhyme of the preceding line: a b a *b b* c b *c c* d c d e e . Yet in spite of the continuity effected by the rhyme, the sonnet breaks into three firm quatrains and a definitive couplet. The initial quatrain argues that grief and remorse are short-lived, the second states that peace inevitably follows pain, and the third quatrain asserts the positive and remedial influence of suffering. Generalizing upon this cycle in the emotional life of man, the concluding couplet urges an acceptance of change or mutation as preferable to "a stable, changeless state." Such a paraphrase is no substitute for the poem, but it does serve to point up Bryant's sensitivity to the structure of progressive quatrains, typical of the sonnet form as it had developed in the work of Shakespeare, Milton, and Wordsworth. Also, it may be suggested that the interlocking rhyme scheme in "Mutation," similar in its effect to the terza rima in English verse, serves to reinforce through the pattern of sounds the theme of gradual and unceasing "mutation." Bryant employs the iambic pentameter line skillfully to convey the tone of optimistic certitude in the first two quatrains, and in order to make his couplet sufficiently reflective, he inserts an additional stress to make an iambic hexameter of the fourteenth line.

Nevertheless, the disciplined voice falters, starting at line eight; it has overreached itself. The transition to rhythms of emergent joy is less than successful, in spite of the vigorous emphasis effected by the heavy consonance of lines 8 to 11. The verse strains for its rhymes in lines 11 and 12, and is nearly overcome by the resultant wordiness and awkwardness. In raising more formal problems than he could successfully handle, Bryant shows in "Mutation" (cited here in full) both his enterprising nature and his limitations as a poetic craftsman:

> They talk of short-lived pleasure—be it so—
>   Pain dies as quickly: stern, hard-featured Pain
> Expires, and lets her weary prisoner go.
>   The fiercest agonies have shortest reign;
>
> And after dreams of horror, comes again
> The welcome morning with its rays of peace.
>   Oblivion, softly wiping out the stain,
> Makes the strong secret pangs of shame to cease:
>
> Remorse is virtue's root; its fair increase
>   Are fruits of innocence and blessedness:
> Thus joy, o'erborne and bound, doth still release
>   His young limbs from the chains that round him press.
>
> Weep not that the world changes—did it keep
> A stable, changeless state, 'twere cause indeed to weep. [15]

Less ambitious in its structure and simpler in its progression of mood is the sonnet "November." Although the quatrains contrast with one another and reinforce the Janus-faced quality which the poet imputes to November, the rhymes are simpler and the rhythm is fairly uniform throughout. The elements of the sonnet form, even though they are not fully exploited here, work harmoniously together to define the lyrical response of the poet to the season:

Yet one smile more, departing, distant sun!
    One mellow smile through the soft vapory air,
Ere, o'er the frozen earth, the loud winds run,
    Or snows are sifted o'er the meadows bare.
One smile on the brown hills and naked trees,
    And the dark rocks whose summer wreaths are cast,
And the blue gentian-flower, that, in the breeze,
    Nods lonely, of her beauteous race the last.
Yet a few sunny days, in which the bee
    Shall murmur by the hedge that skirts the way,
The cricket chirp upon the russet lea,
    And man delight to linger in thy ray.
Yet one rich smile, and we will try to bear
The piercing winter frost, and winds, and darkened air.[16]

The melodic element prevails in "November," much more than it does in "Mutation." The soothing alliterative effects contribute to the mood and, through their distribution of stress, to the rhythm. By his skillful combination of a restricted meter and rhyme with a pervasive musicality, Bryant was able in the sonnet, in the elegy, and in numerous other regular stanzaic patterns to tap the nonrational and simply emotive sources of his creativity. At those points where he permitted the form itself, either traditional or improvised, to bear the responsibilities of order and coherence, Bryant most fully capitalized upon the virtues of his formal voice. Where euphony was permitted to prevail over meaning, his imagination was least inhibited.

Thus the sonnet "To Cole," which relies principally upon its imagery to convey its meaning, sustains its forceful rhythms and its militant harmonies throughout. The structure is implicit in the poem, modestly hiding its logic in thick folds of sensory experience. The sonnet is simply a reminder, addressed directly to the painter, to view the European scenes he is about to visit through the eyes of his early piety, nationalism, and optimism. In observing the picturesque melancholy of cultures eroded by the forces of history— "paths, homes, graves, ruins"—Cole should bear in mind "A living image of our own bright land." Against the imagery of European decay and dissolution, Bryant opposes the vision that Cole had imparted through his huge canvases—of a new world with unsullied open spaces. Without an obtrusive statement to this effect, Bryant draws upon the two accepted denominators of cultivated taste in his day, the "picturesque" and the "sublime," and contrasts them neatly within the limits of the form. One quatrain of exhortation, one quatrain of strident description of the divine wilderness of Cole's canvases, one quatrain of subdued preview of European sights—a thumping heroic couplet restating the exhortation—and a wealth of poetic experience has been condensed into the fourteen lines of "To Cole, the Painter, Departing for Europe":

> Thine eyes shall see the light of distant skies;
>> Yet, Cole! thy heart shall bear to Europe's strand
>> A living image of our own bright land,
> Such as upon thy glorious canvas lies;
>
> Lone lakes—savannas where the bison roves—
>> Rocks rich with summer garlands—solemn streams—
>> Skies, where the desert eagle wheels and screams—
> Spring bloom and autumn blaze of boundless groves.
>
> Fair scenes shall greet thee where thou goest—fair,
>> But different—everywhere the trace of men,
>> Paths, homes, graves, ruins, from the lowest glen
> To where life shrinks from the fierce Alpine air—
>
> Gaze on them, till the tears shall dim thy sight,
> But keep that earlier, wilder image bright. [17]

Similarly, in his use of his classical elegy Bryant relies less upon the structure of ideas than upon the unity imposed by the rhyme and rhythm of the form. In the case of the elegy, the problems are less of rhyme and more of meter, for the basic unit of the eight-foot couplet is easily worked into the conventional quatrain. But the meter of the elegy, as Bryant practiced it, even though the seventh and eighth feet of each couplet asserted a basic iambic pentameter, allowed for considerable substitution in the remaining six feet. For Bryant—who had written in the *North American Review* of 1819 that poetry should avoid "tame iambics" and the "dead waste of dissyllabic feet," and cultivate, instead, "a freer use of trisyllabic feet"[18]—the elegy had the notable advantage of combining a fundamental metrical regularity with a degree of license. Within an elegy, such as "To the Fringed Gentian," Bryant availed himself of his freedom and used effectively both the anapest and spondee without disturbing the smooth movement of the lines. Only two places in "To the Fringed Gentian" reveal Bryant's failure to provide the discipline of the seventh and eighth feet, and both cases can be easily justified by their metrical context. The success of "To the Fringed Gentian" is more than technical, however, and it is the rhythm of temperate despair caught by each successive couplet that combines sound with sense. It is rhythm, more than thought, which builds the quiet tension through the poem and carefully restrains it until the moment of brief, climactic release—"Blue—blue— . . . . ."

The melodies of this poem speak for themselves, yet the principle of symmetrical construction, essential to the classical elegy, deserves comment. Through a combination of alliteration and internal rhyme, Bryant shapes line after line into a delicate fabric of total harmony. The principle of balance may be obvious in a line such as "Thou waitest late and comest alone," but the equilibrium of "The hour of death draw near to me" is less clear until the repeated consonant sounds—*th*, *d*, and *r*,—are distinguished. And the internal rhyme in the line, "The aged *year* is *near* his end," is also easy to overlook in the anticipation of the end rhyme. When variety was needed to break the pattern of the symmetrical line, Bryant was capable of constructing an asymmetrical line of great beauty. The high point of "To a Fringed Gentian," "Blue—blue—as if that sky let fall / A flower from its cerulean wall," is created by an intricate patterning of the repeated vowel sound of *oo*, and the soft consonants *l* and *f*.

One path toward greater lyrical intensity is the shortened poetic line of three or four stresses. Although the pentameter line is generally accepted as the norm for poetry in English, the shorter line has several advantages. It compresses the language, thus demanding more involvement by the reader, it lends itself to suggestive, less explicit expression, and, if used adroitly, it encourages an intensity of emotion. Recent criticism, from feminist critics in particular, has argued that the pentameter line is predominately masculine and thus its use is a "code" for male dominance. How one reconciles this with the fact that most nineteenth-century male poets adapted themselves to the shorter lines to achieve certain effects, is not certain, but it is clear that the shorter line is more muted, gives itself to more subtle expression, and generally suggests a greater degree of intimacy than the more sedate and formal pentameter.

Such is the case in Bryant's hymns, first collected and published
in 1864. He wrote them largely in his early years but continued to
produce them sporadically throughout his career. They were most
often composed in a four-foot line, and many of them follow the
basic metrics of the old New England standby, Watt's *Hymns,*
organized into quatrains of iambic tetrameter, with three-foot lines
interpolated into the stanzas in various patterns. Bryant's hymn "In
Memoriam" (1856), for example, scans according to what was known
as the "common meter," in which the second and fourth line of
each quatrain are shortened to three feet (4 3 4 3):

> Two hundred times has June renewed
> Her roses since the day
> Where here, amid the lonely wood,
> Our fathers met to pray. [19]

The rhythm established here is familiar to church-goers even today
and connotes a delicate pathos and tenderness difficult to achieve
with the pentameter line.

A more heavily stressed hymn, "This Do, in Remembrance of
Me," still gives the effect of the dying fall in the second and fourth
lines:

> All praise to Him of Nazareth
> The Holy One who came
> For love of man, to die a death
> Of agony and shame. [20]

Most of the hymns, however, are composed in regular quatrains
of iambic tetrameter, appropriate to the worship of praise and exaltation. In 1842, Bryant wrote, evidently considering it to be a
hymn, a brief lyric poem that mourns the death of William Ellery
Channing, the preeminent voice of nineteenth-century Unitarianism. Consistent with Channing's message of optimism and hope,
its rhythms have a calm lilt to them and anticipate the message of
joy in the concluding stanza:

> While yet the harvest-fields are white,
> And few the toiling reapers stand,
> Called from his task before the night,
> We miss the mightiest of the band.

> Oh, thou of strong and gentle mind,
>   Thy thrilling voice shall plead no more
> For Truth, for Freedom, and Mankind—
>   The lesson of thy life is o'er.
>
> But thou in brightness, far above
>   The fairest dream of human thought,
> Before the seat of Power and Love,
>   Art with the Truth that thou has sought.[21]

Among his secular poems, a few, such as "A Sick Bed" (1858) and "The Return of the Birds" (1864), actually come close to the traditional hymn meter, but Bryant's more usual practice was simply to establish in the opening lines of his poem a foundation line of three or four feet and then to expand or compress it as the tone or subject matter seemed to require. Thus, "My Autumn Walk" (1865) sets the rhythmic thrust of the three stress line in the first stanza:

> On woodlands ruddy with autumn
>   The amber sunshine lies;
> I look on the beauty round me,
>   And tears come into my eyes.[22]

This meditation on the personal tragedies attendant on the Civil War continues for a full sixteen stanzas that vary considerably in their content and rhythm. Some of them are disconsolate comments on those who have lost sons or husbands, while others present patriotic justifications for this suffering. In a stanza of mourning, for instance, Bryant attenuates the lines and the stresses are muted:

> But who shall comfort the living,
>   The light of whose homes is gone:
> The bride that early widowed,
>   Lives broken-hearted on.

But in the more militant stanzas the trimeter is forcefully asserted:

> Oh, for that better season,
>   When the pride of the foe shall yield
> And the host of God and Freedom
>   March back from the well-worn field.

Most significant in "My Autumn Walk" is that Bryant works against the prevailing metric, discards the iamb in favor of longer feet, closes his lines with feminine endings that are often dangling half feet, and is even willing to overload his line with heavily accented syllables, as he does, for example, in "The mock-grape's blood-red banner." For all the pious and conventional language of the poem, it is an excellent exercise in rhythmic control and illustrates the kind of invention of which Bryant was capable in his use of the shortened line. Other poems show this same craftsmanship. "A Scene on the Banks of the Hudson" (1828) applies a four-foot line to capture the mood of the fugitive poet seeking respite in natural beauty: "River: in this still hour thou hast / Too much of heaven on earth to last."[23]

Not that Bryant's use of the short line was always effective. "A Lifetime" (1876) attempts too much in making the trimeter sustain his nostalgic musings and self-explorations over 148 lines, much too long to sustain the fragile line structure. But it has a few fine moments. The opening stanza, for instance, is nicely paced and sets the reflective mood:

> I sit in the early twilight,
>   And, through the gathering shade,
> I look on the fields around me
>   Where yet a child I played.[24]

And as he looks to the heavens, imagining that his deceased wife appears, his restrained and simple eloquence cuts through the banality of the situation:

> I know the sweet calm features;
>   The peerless smile I know,
> And I stretch my arms with transport
>   From where I stand below.

There is no finer use of the abbreviated line, however, than that in an obscure little verse, a translation from the Spanish of a Mexican poet, José Rosas. In its compression, in its precise diction, and in its rhythmic modulations, "The Cost of Pleasure" invites comparison in its handling of the trimeter line with Emily Dickinson's "I Never Saw a Moor." The metaphor, with its hint of sexuality, is strictly

that of the Mexican poet (and probably did not even occur to Bryant).
But even more than the play upon dew drops and the rose, the
rhyme and rhythm of the translation are what make "The Cost of
Pleasure" work:

> Upon the valley's lap
>   The liberal morning throws
> A thousand drops of dew
>   To wake a single rose.
>
> Thus often, in the course
>   Of life's few fleeting years,
> A single pleasure costs
>   The soul a thousand tears.[25]

Blank Verse

In spite of its value in leading him to the sensuous and suggestive
core of his subject matter, the formal voice, even if perfected, could
not fully realize Bryant's total response to his experience. For the
demands of form and his own limitations made one thing certain:
if he were to cultivate his aesthetic sensibility, he must sacrifice
those intellectual qualities he considered to be essential to noble
and elevated poetry. His respect for the reasoning faculties of the
mind—not, as some might have it, any moral scruples about pleasure—led him into another area of poetic technique where intellect
could have its say. Blank verse had the advantages of scope and
permissiveness, and while Bryant was well aware of the fruits of
metrical discipline, the very breadth and inclusiveness of his experience demanded a more open form.

There are several appropriate ways of considering the technique
of his blank verse, but some are obvious and others are blind alleys.
To say that Bryant drew from a vital tradition of poetry in the
English language—a tradition that runs from Shakespeare through
Milton and down to Wordsworth—contributes little to our understanding of his motivation or of the spirit in which he adopted this
verse form. We know that he was stimulated by Cowper's "The
Task" and that the possibilities for combining natural imagery with
blank verse were further revealed to him by Thomson's *The Seasons*.
But, if books from abroad provided him with certain basic idioms
and perhaps with some of his rhythms, such devices tended to be

the tools of his art rather than its substance. While Bryant appears to have felt secure in the shadow of precedent, his concern was for personal expression—not for the perpetuation of an art form.

Yet in this direction there is not much to guide us. Bryant offers little criticism, or even unpublished correspondence, that suggests what he felt to be the function of blank verse or its place in his own work. His remarks in the *Lectures,* upon which this discussion must draw, are addressed not to the problems of blank verse but to those of poetry as a whole. This critical silence on an important phase of his work, however, is in itself important. For in this area particularly, Bryant preferred to work intuitively. The meticulous craftsmanship of the elegies and of the sonnets reveals a conscious attention to the details of composition, but the blank verse gives every sign of being written whole and revised diffidently. Even the case McDowell makes for Bryant's careful reworking of his material hinges largely upon "Thanatopsis"—which he most certainly did labor over—and upon the formal lyrics.[26] In the body of the blank verse there is little to indicate that Bryant did more than polish the more evident rough spots and attend to flaws in organization.

In practice, the voice that speaks out of the blank verse was conditioned by two dominant influences, neither of them, in any strict sense, poetic. The first of these was Bryant's own prose style, a simplified version of the neoclassical rhetoric. At its worst, the old rhetoric was pedantic, inflated, and intemperate; at its best, it harnessed the forces of wit, logic, and fancy into a well-matched team. In political and religious tracts toward the close of the eighteenth century, this rhetoric strove for an eloquence that would combine rational persuasion with the elevated style of the grand manner. Bryant had pruned from his own prose the more glaring absurdities of the "false sublime," and his own career in journalism further encouraged him toward a more direct, honest expression of thought and feeling.[27] Yet the temper of "eloquence" remained, and its assumed relationship between writer and reader was seldom far from Bryant's mind.

Next to this eloquence, the theory of the "association of ideas" was instrumental in molding the blank verse. From this theory, as subsequent discussion will attempt to make clear, Bryant derived both an articulated justification of what impulse led him to do anyway, and a poetic technique for the management of metaphor and symbol. The act of association, as Bryant adapted it to his own

purposes, became a vehicle for reflective reverie. Conditioned by
the experiences of the past and dependent upon the solitude and
silence of nature for its operation, this voice—perhaps best called
the "voice of eloquent reverie"—would give expression to Bryant's
greatest poem, "Thanatopsis," and to the other major works in
blank verse: "Inscription for the Entrance to a Wood," "The Prairies,"
"Monument Mountain," "The Antiquity of Freedom," and "The
Fountain."

Contributions of Prose Style to the Blank Verse

The prose style Bryant formulated and practiced has a distinctive
voice that yields no hint of a divided or unrealized self. This voice
is fully articulate, consistent, and easily identified. The tone,
rhythms, and diction are invariably those of a person of dignity,
intellect, and character who speaks to his audience from a slightly
elevated podium. In the *Evening Post* and in Bryant's travel accounts
and correspondence, as well as in his public addresses, the platform
manner is never totally in abeyance. No problems of the relationship
of writer to reader obtrude, nor does the attitude of the writer to
his materials present any substantial difficulty. Though the voice
of reason may lapse from time to time into pathos, it does so because
of its high-minded benevolence; if it rises to a pitch of vehement
denunciation, it may be understood to do so because of a legitimate
indignation; when it strikes a few sparks of wit, the reader recognizes
that such levity is an adornment of the educated style.

Whatever the level appropriate to the audience or subject matter,
this prose voice had the capacity for bringing a crystalline clarity
to diffused ideas and for imposing order upon numerous and sometimes complex materials. The confident and reasonable voice of the
editor, traveler, and public speaker imparts its own elevation of
purpose and secures dignity to all that it expresses. This quality of
the voice itself—rather than any specific techniques of persuasion,
any syntactical formulae, or any ground rules for organizing the
prose piece—is what Bryant adopted from the rhetoric learned at
school and college. It is a quality that breathes through imagery
and rhythm, that pervades the tone of each piece, and that he would
use to bring cohesiveness and perspective to the poetry as well as
the prose.

In the travel literature, for example, Bryant communicates precisely and selectively, but he suggests little sense of personal involvement with the places seen or with people whom he met. An extreme instance, dated 19 June 1832, comes from the posthumous *Prose Writings* and tells of his travels through Illinois. During the trip his horse became frightened, "reared and plunged," shook off the saddlebags, then kicked them thoroughly, and ran off, leaving Bryant stranded on the prairie. But in the face of this catastrophe, the writer's style is composed; it almost reaches the point of deadpan comedy:

I now thought my expedition at an end, and had the comfortable prospect of returning on foot or of adopting the method called "to ride and tie." I picked up the saddle-bags and their contents, and, giving them to John, I took charge of the umbrellas, which had also fallen off, and walked back for two miles under a hot sun, when I was met by a man riding a horse, which I was very glad to discover was the one that had escaped.[28]

In a tone of similar detachment he tells of crossing Salt Creek and of watching two travelers forced to swim their horses against the current, one of the men being thrown in transit. He describes the squalor and poverty of a family living in a log cabin on the prairie, and he successfully communicates the experience of lodging there overnight: "The heat of the fire, the stifling atmosphere, the groans and tossings of the sick man, who got up once in fifteen minutes to take medicine or go to the door, the whimperings of the children, and the offensive odors of the place, prevented us from sleeping, and by four o'clock the next morning we had caught and saddled our horses and were on our journey."[29]

Bryant was affected, however, by a few more reactions than gladness and sleeplessness, and a touch of humor graces his dialogue with a Dutch settler, a woman who had provided the travelers with cornbread and milk: "On my saying that I had lived among the Dutch in New York and elsewhere, she remarked that she reckoned that was the reason why I did not talk like a Yankee. I replied that no doubt living among the Dutch had improved my English."[30]

Or in his *Letters* telling of a trip to Illinois in 1841, there is this passage—one of several—depicting the natural attractiveness of the countryside: "From the door of one of these dwellings I surveyed a prospect of exceeding beauty. The windings of the river allowed us a sight of its waters and its beautifully diversified banks to a great distance each way, and in one direction a high prairie region was seen above the woods that fringed the course of this river, of a lighter green than they, and touched with the golden light of the setting sun."[31]

Yet always the voice is that of the literate, cosmopolitan gentleman who may observe, note, and express a few pertinent sentiments without fully engaging himself in the flow of life. It is a subjective voice in that the articulate self always remains apart from the experience it encounters. For all its apparent nonpartisan objectivity, it lacks true objectivity—that which respects the integrity and complexity of outward things and that seeks, as the natural scientist seeks, to probe their inner meanings, their causes, and their relationships. This subjective voice, which could speak endlessly of experience as though it were a vast, unrolling panorama, while maintaining its own pedestal unscarred by events, is the voice that speaks also in the blank verse.

Closer to the blank verse in its elevated tone, however, is the language of Bryant's formal orations. The most noted of these were the memorial discourses in which Bryant recounted the lives and assessed the achievements of his deceased contemporaries. Despite the impressionistic vagueness of many of his remarks (Washington Irving, for example, is described as "the best-natured and most amiable of satirists"[32]), Bryant offered to his audiences a wealth of information on lives and works, an impressive accumulation of significant quotations, and a relatively balanced appraisal of men and their works. The carefully directed passages of pathos or irony are generally subordinate to the central tone of sympathetic seriousness. A few metaphors are permitted to appear in order to unite the loosely structured discussion, and in this, as much as in anything, lies the difference between the addresses and the descriptive prose. One such metaphor conveys the ponderous force of a Cooper novel as it slowly develops:

The progress of the plot, at first, is like that of one of his own vessels of war, slowly, heavily, and even awkwardly working out of a harbour. We are impatient and weary, but when the vessel is once in the open sea, and feels the free breath of heaven in her full sheets, our delight and admiration are all the greater at the grace, the majesty and power with which she divides and bears down the waves, and pursues her course, at will, over the great waste of waters.[33]

Recognizable in this passage are several elements of Bryant's blank verse: the generalized and dignified diction, the rhythms of the parallel constructions building toward a contrived climax, and the closing image of an immense and immortal nature. This voice—which could clothe an acute critical observation in an elocutionary rhetoric and evoke not merely the rational respect due to a work of art but also a true sense of "delight and admiration" as the critic has felt it—was the voice readily adapted to poetry, particularly to poetry that permitted the platform posturing and the full-chested rhythms of praise and exultation.

Contributions of Associationism to the Blank Verse

What the prose voice could not provide for the blank verse, however, was the free flow between observation and reflection, between the external events witnessed and recorded and the internal reactions of heart and mind to these events. While the prose voice stood stolidly in the midst of multiple sensations, permitting itself only parenthetical expressions of feeling or thought, the poetic voice was compelled by its own nature to seek fullness of expression even at the risk of disunity.

Bryant had found in his reading in Reid and Stewart, the two leading exponents of the associational movement in British philosophy, an account of how the mind receives and interprets its experiences; even more important for his poetry was his discovery in Archibald Alison's *Essays on the Nature and Principles of Taste* (1790) of the significant role the imagination might play.[34] Alison offered to the young poet not only a justification for his reveries but also a prescription for a freer poetry. When Bryant presented the notion of "suggestion" in his *Lectures,* he was not only making a basic point about his own poetry but was also echoing Alison, who had said that "The object itself appears only to serve as a hint, to awaken the imagination and to lead it through every analogous idea that has its place in the memory." When Alison wrote of the succession of ideas that physical objects serve to stimulate as "trains of pleasing and solemn thought arising spontaneously within our minds,"[35] he put the seal of critical approval upon the device used by Bryant in "Thanatopsis," in "Inscription for the Entrance to a Wood," in "The Antiquity of Freedom," and in "The Fountain" whereby the

narrator of the poem enters upon the natural scene and—under its
influence—lets his mind turn inward upon himself or backward in
time.

The advantages of the "association of ideas," in the sense which
Alison developed the concept, were clearly those needed by Bryant.
He must have been aware, of course, of Wordsworth's successful
use of reminiscence in "Tintern Abbey" and other poems, and thus
he cannot be considered, even in his early blank verse, as an in-
novator. But from Alison, and perhaps from Wordsworth, he found
a psychological basis upon which he could structure his poems.
Neither formal rhyme schemes nor the rhetoric of eloquence could
provide him with an intrinsic order, for both were essentially forms
of order imposed upon thought and feeling from the outside—from
traditional prosody, from the rule books, from the accepted canons
of taste. The association of ideas was not, of course, a stream of
consciousness, but then respectable poets of the early nineteenth
century did not acknowledge the vulgar rumblings of the id. They
did recognize, however, that there were ineffable truths not touched
by the recognized thought of their time, that the reflective process
consisted of much more than conditioned responses to beauty as it
was visualized centuries before in places thousands of miles away.
And while, as an editor, Bryant appreciated the role of language in
its argumentative and persuasive capacities, he also understood the
human need for forms of order expressive of the autonomous self.

The association of ideas, as Bryant understood it, placed the
individual face to face with the simple realities and divine order in
nature and then allowed matters to take their course. The "structure"
of the poems was the dynamic structure of the dialogue between
man and Nature. That the reverie generally turned to the past and
that the successive images (as in "The Fountain") reveal the history
of man from his primitive times were clear indications that nature's
great principle of temporal change was communicated to the poet.
That the reverie would often bring to light conflicting points of
view (as in "The Antiquity of Freedom") was a sign of nature's
transcendence over petty man. That the structure of each of the
poems in blank verse develops according to its own particular needs
(as in "Thanatopsis" or "Summer Wind") signifies the spontaneous
quality of each creative experience and the diversity of forms which
the dialogue between man and nature may take.

If the ideas of association psychology had led Bryant to a more flexible organization for the blank verse, they also brought him to a reconsideration of metaphor and symbol. In a significant passage in the *Lectures* he speaks of "analogies and correspondences" in a manner that anticipates the more sophisticated handling of the problem a decade later in the fourth chapter of Emerson's *Nature:*

Among the most remarkable of the influences of poetry is the exhibition of those analogies and correspondences which it beholds between the things of the moral and of the natural world. I refer to its adorning and illustrating each by the other—infusing a moral sentiment into natural objects, and bringing images of visible beauty and majesty to heighten the effect of moral sentiment. Thus it binds into one all the passages of human life and connects all the varieties of human feeling within the work of creation.[36]

At their worst, these "analogies," as they occur in Bryant's poetry, could be contrived and sentimental. Sometimes they come within the sights of the "pathetic fallacy," for which Ruskin castigated the romantics. But, at its best, the analogy could be "suggestive" and could break out of the pattern of explicit or stereotyped metaphor. Consistent with the emphasis of Alison, the analogies could rise spontaneously within the poet's mind as his eye rested upon the natural objects appropriate to his solemn and pleasing thoughts.

These analogies were not, of course, limited to the blank verse. "To the Fringed Gentian," "The Death of the Flowers," "To Cole," and "To the Apennines" illustrate how Bryant infused and heightened moral sentiment within the pattern of conventional rhymes. The blank verse, however, in its less restricted outpouring of poetic ideas, carried to a further extreme the binding "into one all the passages of human life." The fine line that generally divides imagery from metaphor becomes gently obscured as all the phenomena of nature assume the task of suggestion. Observation and reflection, sensuous joy and moral insight blend into one another until the critical task of analysis becomes difficult indeed. A poem like "Monument Mountain" explains itself to some extent, and the analogy between the mountain and human aspiration can be traced through the passages of narration and description. But in "The Prairies" the analogy is less clear, and the prairies suggest a number of relevant ideas with no central thread upon which they can be strung. And in "The Fountain" we are well within the realm of the obscure where meanings lie remote beneath the surface and are fair game only for persevering critics.

"The Painted Cup"

By way of illustration, a relatively short poem in blank verse, "The Painted Cup," tells us more than a fragment of the better-known poems does. A poem about ways of seeing, it is comparable in its play of perspectives to Wallace Stevens's "Thirteen Ways of Looking at a Blackbird." The infusion of moral sentiment is restrained; the imagery is suggestive within an inclusive framework of meaning. All in all, the poem shows Bryant at his figurative best, for each step in his train of associations contributes to a total perception of this prairie flower.

The first way of seeing is that of the "wanderer": the "dilated eye" through which Bryant himself had first seen the prairies. The vision is pictorial, and each detail is composed within the frame of the vista:

> The fresh savannas of the Sangamon
> Here rise in gentle swells, and the long grass
> Is mixed with rustling hazels. Scarlet tufts
> Are glowing in the green, like the flakes of fire;
> The wanderers of the prairie know them well,
> And call that brilliant flower the Painted Cup.

At this point the strophe breaks and Bryant addresses the reader. He refers to a point made at length in the *Lectures* —that the older mythologies are inapplicable within the world revealed by empirical science:

> Now, if thou art a poet, tell me not
> That these bright chalices were tinted thus
> To hold the dew for fairies, when they meet
> On moonlight evenings in the hazel-bowers,
> And dance till they are thirsty. Call not up,
> Amid this fresh and virgin solitude,
> The faded fancies of an elder world . . .

Here the verse, without a break in syntax, launches into the third way of seeing, the empathetic apprehension of the flowers within the natural processes of their environment:

> But leave these scarlet cups to spotted moths
> Of June, and glistening flies, and humming-birds,

> To drink from, when on all these boundless lawns
> The morning sun looks hot. Or let the wind
> O'erturn in sport their ruddy brims, and pour
> A sudden shower upon the strawberry-plant,
> To swell the reddening fruit that even now
> Breathes a slight fragrance from the sunny slope.

Again a shift—another "But"—a relaxing of the strong-stress iambics—and the fourth way of seeing is suggested:

> But thou art of a gayer fancy. Well—
> Let then the gentle Manitou of flowers,
> Lingering amid the bloomy waste he loves,
> Though all his swarthy worshippers are gone—
> Slender and small, his rounded cheek all brown
> And ruddy with the sunshine; let him come
> On summer mornings, when the blossoms wake,
> And part with little hands the spiky grass,
> And touching, with his cherry lips, the edge
> Of these bright beakers, drain the gathered dew. [37]

If mythologies are needed, runs the thought of these closing lines,
let them be those of the American aborigines, and let the poet retain
the freshness and purity of the primitive imagination.

In "The Painted Cup" Bryant exploited to its fullest the speculative freedom bestowed upon him by the doctrine of the association
of ideas. Not only does the use of metaphor and symbol rise above
the mechanical comparisons that characterize the lesser poets of any
era, but the rhythms themselves, like those of all of his better blank
verse, are those of the mind itself as it ponders and meditates. The
preponderance of run-on lines, the abundant caesuras, the natural
syncopation that occurs when the voice inclines toward a regular
pattern of stresses—all these elements contribute to the rich sonority
and high seriousness of Bryant's great works in blank verse. At a
further range from the deliberate musicality of the formal lyrics lie
the spontaneous rhythms and chance harmonies of these lines. The
touches of alliteration, such as those in the line "A sudden shower
on a strawberry plant," may contribute to the pervasive sibilance
of a passage; elsewhere they may bring an intensification of stress
in a particular line, such as "The faded fancies of an elder world";
but the patterns of sound are generally subordinate to the rhythm

and to the imagery as they develop through the poem. The blank verse placed a premium on the action of the intellect, and only those sensuous elements that could cooperate with the movement of thought find a place in this verse.

The Pitfalls of Blank Verse

If the blank verse drew from these two sources, and was indeed the "voice of eloquent revery," its continued success depended upon a delicate coordination. This is the irony of Bryant's style. While the rhetoric of eloquence could provide him with a stable center for his creative activity, it could also leave his expression vaporous, void of content, and out of touch with his listeners. Though the association of ideas might secure for him the freedom and inwardness that brought his poetry to life, it could easily become a stylistic trick—and one without relevance either to his deeper thoughts or to the eternal truths of nature. Even in the blank verse of his middle periods—"Earth" (1834), for example—the rhetorical effects could take over and not only leave the language flaccid but also detract from the smooth and suggestive train of ideas. And, as a previous chapter has pointed out, the association of ideas becomes an inert principle once the sense of communion with nature is lost. Thus, while "Among the Trees" (1868) has many fine lines, its language gradually loses contact with any substantial reality; the poem therefore concludes lamely with a banal figure that might easily have been drawn from an eighteenth-century political tract:

> The hand of ruffian Violence, that now
> Is insolently raised to smite, shall fall
> Unnerved before the calm rebuke of Law,
> And Fraud, his sly confederate, shrink, in shame,
> Back to his covert, and forego his prey.[38]

As a poet, Bryant is no exceptional case; for any creative artist, the pitfalls lie on all sides. If he had bad habits impressed upon him during his back-country education, he made the most of them. If his reading in British literature and philosophy opened up promising new vistas for him, these insights too quickly became mannerisms. Though he developed an extraordinary ear for the musical effects of language early in his career, these very effects militated against the full articulation of his thought. Though he claimed to speak authoritatively for the role of imagination in literature, his aptitude lay not in the creation of startling new effects and prophetic questions but rather in the restatement of old truths and in the resolution of contemporary crises of the heart and mind.

To say that Bryant spoke with a divided voice is an essential criticism, but it need not be a severe one. Along each of the trails that he tramped alone, he left a number of memorable literary landmarks. Nor was his failure absolute, depending as it does upon our assessment of his talent. If we take his best poems, however, as a true index of his ability, he falls short of his own standard of achievement. Unable to assess himself completely as a poet, unwilling to formulate the fast, guiding principles by which his genius would be directed, and uncompromising in his attachment to the two divergent paths along which he was wont to stray, Bryant failed to realize that distinctive originality which is the mark of the great poets of his day and ours.

Chapter Seven
"The Dear Old Poet"

A member of the literary colony summering in the Berkshires in 1850 recalled years later a curious tribute that the group made to a one-time native of the area. The incident, related by James T. Fields, concerned a toast offered during a picnic on a mountaintop. The object of the toast was William Cullen Bryant; among the toasters were Hawthorne, Holmes, Melville, and Duyckinck: ". . . Then we all assembled in a shady spot, and one of the party read to us Bryant's beautiful poem commemorating 'Monument Mountain.' Then we lunched among the rocks, and somebody proposed Bryant's health, and 'long life to the dear old poet.' This was the most popular toast of the day, and it took, I remember, a considerable amount of Heidsieck to do it justice."[1]

Few sophisticated readers will miss the lingering hint of irony— even for modern ears—in this sentimental adulation of the rising generation for "the dear old poet." Bryant was, first of all, neither "old" relative to the group, nor was he plausibly "dear." On that August day of 1850 he was still vigorously editing the *Evening Post,* he was only fifty-five years of age, and he was merely ten years in advance of Hawthorne himself. As for his being "dear" to any of the group—it seems unlikely.

On the other hand, there is little reason to believe that any deliberate sarcasm was intended. "Monument Mountain" was an appropriate poem for the occasion, and its theme of illicit passion might well have affected the authors of *Pierre* and *The Scarlet Letter.* Bryant is not known to have given offense to any of those present, either as a political writer or as a literary critic. Nor did he, as an artist, pose any serious threat to their literary fortunes. His best-known poems had been published decades before ("Thanatopsis" antedated Herman Melville's birth by two years), and his output during the 1840s presented no serious challenge to anyone. In a sense, he had become a very comfortable institution in American letters—merely a reminder that poetry could flourish in American culture. If Bryant as a man or as an artist was not literally a "dear old poet," he, as a representative man of letters, certainly struck the rising generation as being both distantly congenial and also conveniently passé.

Reaction

Bryant symbolized for them, of course, a definite and concluded stage in the progress toward a national literature. Within a very few days of this expedition Melville was to write his famous review of Hawthorne's *Mosses* in which he claimed to have discovered on native ground a genius comparable to that of Shakespeare. Hawthorne, wrote Melville, had the power to "probe to the very axis of reality." Like Shakespeare, he could capture the quality of "blackness" and portray "the sane madness of vital truth."[2]

If Melville's gesture was characteristically grandiose, it still made clear the distinction between the generation of Bryant, Cooper, and Irving, and that of Hawthorne, Melville, Poe, Thoreau, and Whitman. In order for the second growth of probers, seekers, and prophets to arise, the old elms had to be transplanted from the creative ground. The new catchwords of "genius," "spirit," "daemonic," and "intuition" in a few years undid the works of lifetimes. The new Sturm und Drang could well afford to patronize the less frenzied, less pessimistic, less lyrically irrational artists in whose shade they had been nurtured. The very notion of literary nationalism in America implied a perpetually forward sweep of the creative wave. It was not, after all, the fault of the emergent authors that Bryant had not gracefully removed himself, as Cooper and Irving had done, when his contribution was essentially finished. Yet by patronizing him the same end was accomplished. A few kind critical paragraphs, a jovial toast in Heidsieck, and the shadows of past creative effort were dispelled.

Emerson, Poe, and Whitman each contributed a favorable word or two toward these critical obsequies. Even as early as 1839 Emerson was writing off the entire previous generation, saying that "all the American geniuses . . . Irving, Bryant, Greenough, Everett, Channing, even Webster in his recorded Eloquence, all lack nerve and dagger."[3] Again in 1844 an entry in Emerson's *Journals* identifies Bryant with an era of creativity which had somehow failed: "But in America I grieve to miss the strong black blood of the English race: ours is a pale diluted stream. What a company of brilliant

young persons I have seen with so much expectation! the sort is
very good, but none is good enough of his sort. Every one an
imperfect specimen; respectable, not valid. Irving thin, and Channing thin, and Bryant and Dana; Prescott and Bancroft . . . ."[4]

Appreciation

Yet Emerson was also the most perceptive of readers. He recognized the worth of the poet to the extent of including him on
the faculty of an imaginary "ideal" college,[5] and he found solid
value in the poems themselves: "Bryant has learned where to hang
his titles, namely by tying his mind to autumn woods, winter
mornings, rain, brooks, mountains, evening winds, and wood-birds.
Who speaks of these is forced to remember Bryant. [He is] American. Never despaired of the Republic. Dared name a jay and a
gentian, crows also. His poetry is sincere."[6]
    Thus, once Emerson had vented his lamentations over the state
of genius in America, he could come round to an implied acknowledgment of what his generation owed to the previous one. As his
quotation illustrates, the debt was threefold: the love of nature,
loyalty to the democratic way of life, and a rugged integrity. After
all, the writer of *Nature, The American Scholar,* and *Self-Reliance* could
hardly ignore the very virtues that he had been preaching. Although
Emerson might have missed the qualities of intellectual enterprise
and imaginative daring in Bryant's poetry, he responded to the
purposeful, moral tone. While the creative dialogue of Bryant's
nature poems may have been something less than Emerson's "original
relation to the universe," still the voice and the posture had much
in common. And if Bryant's commonplace language was no match
for the charged and fiery eloquence that Emerson and his peers had
learned from Edward Everett at Harvard, at least it made occasional
contact with the honest vernacular of the people.
    While Emerson's praise was genuine enough, he made no gesture
toward a rehabilitation of Bryant's reputation by the standards of
the mid-century. Poe, on the other hand, seriously worried over the
problem of Bryant's "genius." In a critical essay on Bryant's poetry,
Edgar Allan Poe defended those "accuracies and elegancies of style"
characteristic of Bryant's poetry, and he maintained that such "artistic skill" was not entirely incompatible with the profounder qualities of soul and mind. Poe asserted, in the face of the prevailing

estimate, that "Mr. Bryant has genius, and that of a marked character, but it has been overlooked by modern schools, because deficient in those externals which have become in a measure symbolical of those schools." Yet even in his role as apologist, Poe admitted that "It will never do to claim for Bryant a genius of the loftiest order."[7] For reasons never fully developed in his criticism, Poe conceived of at least two distinct ranks of genius, and he generally spoke of Bryant as one comfortably ensconced in the lower rank.

Among Bryant's more sympathetic critics, Whitman was the most extravagant in his praise—and the last to speak out. In a passage from *Specimen Days* titled "My Tribute to Four Poets," he describes the qualities of Bryant's verse in such a way that the unspoken compliment of literary indebtedness is forcefully implied:

Bryant pulsing the first interior verse—throbs of a mighty world—bard of the river and wood, ever conveying a taste of the open air, with scents as from hay fields, grapes, birch-borders—always lurking fond of threnodies—beginning and ending his long career with chants of death, with here and there through all, poems or passages of poems, touching the highest universal truths, enthusiasms, duties—morals as grim and eternal, if not as stormy and fateful, as anything in Aeschylus.[8]

From the perspective of British literary culture, Bryant and his poetry were hopeful signs that the former colonies were attaining some measure of culture. Harriet Martineau had met Bryant on her trip through the States, and in her book *Society in America* she announced that "America has a poet." She saw him more in terms, however, of his potential than his accomplishments, a somewhat ironic observation in 1837 considering that Bryant's poetic powers would shortly begin to wane.

Bryant has not done anything like what he can and will do; but he has done some things that will live. Those of his poems which are the best known, or the most quoted, are smooth, sweet, faithful descriptions of nature, such as his own imagination delights in. . . . If he would live for his gifts, if his future years could be devoted to "clear poetical activity," "looking up," like the true artist, "to his dignity and his calling," that dignity and that calling may prove to be as lofty as they no doubt appeared in the reveries of his boyhood; and he may be listened to as lovingly over the expanse of future time, as he already is over that of the ocean.[9]

Of a lesser order, but each fascinating in its own way, were three
poetic tributes to Bryant, the poet. The most familiar is, of course,
James Russell Lowell's "A Fable for Critics" (1848). Lowell has a
jolly time with what he perceives as Bryant's cool dignity and
Olympian impassivity: "There is no doubt he stands in supreme
iceolation." Following thirty lines of witty invective on this theme,
Lowell ridicules the claim of "some scholar who's hourly expecting
his learning," that Bryant is the "American Wordsworth." He then
moves on, with trenchant insight, to compare Bryant with Cowper
and Thomson, the eighteenth-century British poets who had so
influenced Bryant's poetry in his youth:

> There's T.'s love of nature, C.'s penchant to preach;
> Just mix up their minds so that C.'s spice of craziness
> Shall balance and neutralize T.'s turn for laziness,
> And it gives you a brain cool, quite frictionless, quiet,
> Whose internal police nips the buds of all riot.

Lowell concludes, however, with a compliment to Bryant, which,
however, is not without its own equivocation:

> If I call him an iceburg, I don't mean to say
> There is nothing in that which is grand in its way;
> He is almost the one of your poets that knows,
> How much grace, strength and dignity lie in repose;
> If he sometimes falls short, he is too wise to mar
> His thought's modest fulness by going too far.[10]

Given the context in which Lowell "roasted" all of the prominent
writers of the era, it is useless to complain that Lowell oversimplified
Bryant and his poetry. That "grace, strength and dignity" made
Bryant exceptional in his time tells more about the changes of taste
under way in the 1840s than it tells us about Bryant as a poet.

In stark contrast, both in its elevated tone and in its appraisal of
Bryant, is Bayard Taylor's "Epicedium—William Cullen Bryant"
(1878). Written just a few months after Bryant's death, this funeral
ode is believed to be Taylor's last poem, upon which he labored as
he approached his own demise. Running to well over a hundred
lines, the funeral ode is recognizably prolix and convoluted. Nevertheless, it pays honest homage to Bryant for his immortalizing of

the American natural scenery, "stream and tree, bird and mountain crest," and his lifelong love of freedom—"his last word, as his first was Liberty!" The concluding lines are an eloquent tribute:

> He bowed to wisdom other than his own,
> To wisdom and to law,
> Concealed or dimly shown
> In all he knew not, all he knew and saw,
> Trusting the Present, tolerant of the Past,
> Firm-faithed in what shall come
> When the vain noises of these days are dumb;
> And his first word was noble as his last.[11]

A third poetic tribute is by a minor German poet, Niclas Müller, who may have emigrated to New York in the 1850s. Bryant had translated one of his poems, "Thränenparadies" as "The Paradise of Tears," published in *Graham's Magazine* in 1843. Müller's collection of his verses, *Neure Lieder und Gedichte*, was published in New York in 1867. For all its inflated sentiments, the poem does recognize Bryant as a kindred spirit who reached out beyond his parochial culture and caught the essence of a foreign poet's verse. The poem is, of course, in German, but I here provide a *Nachdictung:*

> To Wm. Cullen Bryant
> Upon Reading His Translation
> Of my "Paradise of Tears"
>
> Through your poetic garden I wander
> And from your flower beds I come
> So many kinds of shining flowers—
> Truely, a poet's herbarium.
>
> As I gaze, in my awe profound,
> And discover in this shade delight,
> In the midst of foliage all around,
> Startling beauties catch my sight.
>
> Now I find one certain flower,
> Barely recalled from long ago,
> For she has donned a different garment,
> And who she is, I do not know.

As my tears begin to swell,
    And I ask how she appears.
She replies I know her well,
    "I am your 'Paradise of Tears.' "

"My dear master has brought me here,
    From his heart, from far away.
He has loved me, well and dear,
    And robed me thus, in this array."

Well, now it is my task, my friend,
    For my tears to make repayment—
As my revenge, "Westwind," I send
    For you to wear, this German raiment.

Bear it in every foreign town,
    Until your crime will be eclipsed!
By it, Westwind, you will be known
    As by the flowers you have kissed. [12]

Toward a Modern Appreciation of Bryant

These tributes and criticisms are of interest because of what they
say about nineteenth-century taste and values. But no matter how
deeply Bryant's contemporaries may have responded to his poetry,
they offer little help to the twentieth-century reader. Whitman's
heady praise leads us to the open-shirt bard of Camden rather than
to the one who prompted his threnodies. Poe's good-but-not-great
evaluation has led subsequent critics to award Bryant a dignified
post in the second rank. [13] Emerson's approval of his sincerity and
pastoral subject matter has kept alive a genteel interest in Bryant's
poems, but it has been as successful in later days as it was in the
1840s in precluding intelligent curiosity on the part of the common
reader. For many years Bryant's fate was in the hands of the ped-
agogues and researchers. The one inflicted long passages of "Thanatopsis" upon the startled minds of the young, the other has searched
for signs of a "usable past" in Bryant's scientism, or patriotism, or
liberalism, or other *isms* easily derived from the poems.

Recent decades have seen a renewed interest in Bryant as a public
figure, and another generation of scholars has discovered a challenge
in his poetry. The well-researched biography by Charles Brown, the

collected *Letters* by Bryant and Voss, and the Centennial Conference of 1978 are signs of renewed interest in this versatile and remarkable man. Recent criticism has examined the poetry for both its rhetoric and its ideas, and the small book in which twenty contemporary poets present their reactions to Bryant is heartening. Yet there is no recent scholarly edition of the poems, and except for letters the prose writings are almost totally ignored.

We have little excuse, with the corporate and mass media sensibility well advanced, to continue in our lethargy and our confusion. The life of poetry has its own integrity. A poet like Bryant can speak to us if we allow ourselves to listen. He may require that we imagine the world as he saw it, but then he permits us to share, to the limits of our capacity, those ecstatic and insightful moments recorded in his poems.

Though we no longer demand with the same urgency that the poet speak for "universal" values, the claim of art as it passes down from generation to generation remains the same. The successful lyric poem is a distillation as well as a crystallization of immediate and personal life. The poet's message goes beyond causes or certitudes; it is a promise of visions and values as yet unrealized in ourselves. To overlook the basic enterprise of a poet like Bryant is to lose our own sense of the inestimable importance of art in our lives, and eventually it is to lose our senses of language, form, and beauty as well.

But we do not claim either "genius" or "greatness" for William Cullen Bryant. Let us, as critics and thoughtful readers, leave these matters of prestige and rank to those who find them important. Certainly we can place a high estimate upon his various accomplishments and yet with clear eyes analyze his limitations and his failures. To examine the quandary we have called his "divided voice" can hardly be taken as a denial that poems in either of his voices— "Thanatopsis" and "To the Fringed Gentian," for example—are triumphs of his art. Nor need we apologize for those aspects of his work that strike us as banal, tendentious, or obscure.

Recognizing the circumstances under which he composed his verse and the standards to which he aspired, we can forgive, and easily forget, the works of lesser significance for us. What we cannot overlook, however, is the noble attempt of the man to forge out of the scraps of an impoverished culture the rails along which men might travel toward a more beautiful and satisfying future. The worst of his poems stand as tokens of expected fulfillment. The best are declarations that the human sensibility can rise independent and vigorous in a new land.

Notes and References

Chapter One

1. "The Poet" (1863; *Thirty Poems*). The text of this and of most of the poems quoted is from *The Poetical Works of William Cullen Bryant* (New York: D. Appleton & Co., 1876). This final edition of the poems was collected and arranged by Bryant and has been generally accepted as the authoritative text. The poems taken from this source will be hereafter noted only by title, by the presumed date of composition, and by the place and date of original publication, as above. Poems not appearing in this 1876 edition are, however, fully documented.

2. Parke Godwin, *A Biography of William Cullen Bryant, with Extracts from His Private Correspondence,* 2 vols. (New York: D. Appleton & Co.), 1:6–28.

3. Ibid., 1:28–37.

4. "A Lifetime" (1876; *Poetical Works,* 1876).

5. "Reminiscences of the 'Evening Post,' by William Cullen Bryant (Extracted from the *Evening Post* of November 15, 1851, with additions and corrections by the writer)" in John Bigelow, *William Cullen Bryant,* American Men of Letters Series (Boston: Houghton Mifflin Co., 1890), 312–42.

6. Allan Nevins, *The Evening Post: A Century of Journalism* (New York: Boni and Liveright, 1922), 350.

7. Ibid., 351.

8. "In Memory of William Leggett" (1839; *Democratic Review,* 1839). "In Memory of John Lothrop Motley" (1877; *International Review,* 1877) in *Poetical Works* (1883) 2:349. "To Cole, the Painter, Departing for Europe" (1829; *Talisman,* 1830).

9. *The New England Magazine* as quoted in Nevins, *Evening Post,* 137.

10. Godwin, *Biography,* 1:334.

11. Bigelow, *Bryant,* 194.

12. *The Letters of William Cullen Bryant* ed. William Cullen Bryant II and Thomas G. Voss, 4 vols. (New York: Fordham University Press, 1975–1984), 1:89.

13. "The Poet" (1863; *Thirty Poems,* 1864).

14. *Selections from Ralph Waldo Emerson: An Organic Anthology,* Riverside Editions, ed. Stephen E. Whicher (Boston: Houghton Mifflin Co., 1957), 168.

15. Godwin, *Biography*, 1:4, 57–58.
16. Ibid., 1:9.
17. Ibid., 1:77–78. See also Tremaine McDowell, "The Juvenile Verse of William Cullen Bryant," *Studies in Philology* 26 (1929):96–116.
18. McDowell, "The Juvenile Verse," 114.
19. Godwin, *Biography*, 1:27.
20. Tremaine McDowell, *William Cullen Bryant*, American Writers Series (New York: American Book Co., 1935), xxv, cites James Grant Wilson, *Bryant and His Friends* (New York, 1885), 430, as the source for this information.
21. Godwin, *Biography*, 1:33.
22. "To a Waterfowl" (1815; *North American Review*, 1818). For a discussion of the date of composition see William Cullen Bryant II, "The Waterfowl in Retrospect," *New England Quarterly* 30 (1957):181–89.
23. Richard Wilbur, "A Word from Cummington," in *William Cullen Bryant and His America: Centennial Conference Proceedings, 1878–1978*, ed. Stanley Brodwin, Michael D'Innocenzo, Joseph P. Astman, (New York: AMS Press, 1983), 32.
24. Henry A. Pochman, *German Culture in America* (Madison: University of Wisconsin Press, 1961), 724. See also A. H. Herrick, "W.C. Bryant's Bezeihungen zur deutschen Dichtung," *Modern Language Notes* 32 (June 1917):344–51.
25. See Donald A. Ringe, "Bryant's Fiction: The Problem of Perception," in Brodwin, *Centennial Conference*, 167–77.
26. "From the Fifth Book of Homer's Odyssey" (1863; *Atlantic Monthly*, 1865).

Chapter Two

1. Editor's Note, *Poetical Works* (1883), 1:351.
2. "The Prairies" (1832; *Knickerbocker Magazine*, 1833). Cf. Ralph N. Miller, "Nationalism in Bryant's 'The Prairies,' " *American Literature* 21 (1949):227–32.
3. Herman Melville was to underscore these lines in his volume of the *Poems* (New York, 1863): Jay Leyda, *The Melville Log*, 2 vols. (New York: Harcourt, Brace & Co.), 2:692.
4. "Earth" (1834; New York *Mirror*, 1835).
5. George Arms, "William Cullen Bryant: A Respectable Station on Parnassus," *University of Kansas City Review* 15 (1949):219–21. My discussion is indebted to this article. For a different perspective see Gaines McMartin, "Patterns of Enclosure: Unity in the Poems of William Cullen Bryant," in Brodwin, *Centennial Conference*, 100.
6. "The Yellow Violet" (1814; *Poems*, 1832).
7. "To the Fringed Gentian" (1829; *Poems*, 1832).

8. "The Death of the Flowers" (1825; *New York Review*, 1825).
9. See A. R. C. Finch, "Dickinson and Patriarchal Meter: A Theory of Metrical Codes," *PMLA* 102 (March 1987):166–76.
10. "Oh Fairest of the Rural Maids" (1820; *Poems*, 1832).
11. "Rizpah" (1824; *United States Literary Gazette*, 1824).
12. "The Maiden's Sorrow" (1842; *Home Library*, 1842).
13. "Monument Mountain" (1824; *United States Literary Gazette*, 1824).
14. "Sella" (1862; *Thirty Poems*, 1864).
15. "The Earth is Full of Thy Riches" (1820), in *Poetical Works* (1883), 2:203.
16. Howard Mumford Jones, *Belief and Disbelief in American Literature* (Chicago: University of Chicago Press, 1967), 38.
17. "A Forest Hymn" (1815; *North American Review*, 1817).
18. "Inscription for the Entrance to a Wood" (1815; *North American Review*, 1817).
19. "A Summer Ramble" (1826; New York *Mirror*, 1826).
20. "Hymn of the City" (1830; *Christian Examiner*, 1830).
21. "The Old Man's Counsel" (1840; *Democratic Review*, 1840).
22. "Among the Trees" (1868; *Putnam's Magazine*, 1869).
23. "The Order of Nature" (1866; Poems, 1871).

Chapter Three

1. "Thanatopsis" (1815–21; *North American Review*, 1817; *Poems*, 1821). The dating of this poem is discussed subsequently in this chapter.
The basic points regarding Bryant's revision of "Thanatopsis" can be observed in the following text of the poem (from *Poetical Works*, 1876). I have italicized those portions added to the main body of the poem subsequent to its original publication in the *North American Review* of 1817. While the opening seventeen lines were not composed until the poet's visit to Cambridge in 1821, the section starting with line 66 had its origins in Manuscript B, ca. 1818. For a detailed study of the various texts see Tremaine McDowell, "Bryant's Practice in Composition and Revision," *Publications of the Modern Language Association* 52 (June 1937): 474–502.

THANATOPSIS

To him who in the love of Nature holds
Communion with her visible forms, she speaks
A various language; for his gayer hours
She has a voice of gladness, and a smile
And eloquence of beauty, and she glides

Into his darker musings, with a mild
And healing sympathy, that steals away
The sharpness, ere he is aware. When thoughts
Of the last bitter hour come like a blight
Over thy spirit, and sad images
Of the stern agony, and shroud, and pall,
And breathless darkness, and the narrow house,
Make thee to shudder, and grow sick at heart;—
Go forth, under the open sky, and list
To Nature's teachings, while from all around—
Earth and her waters, and the depths of air—
Comes a still voice—Yet a few days, and thee
The all-beholding sun shall see no more
In all his course; nor yet in the cold ground,
Where thy pale form was laid, with many tears,
Nor in the embrace of ocean, shall exist
Thy image. Earth, that nourished thee, shall claim
Thy growth, to be resolved to earth again,
And, lost each human trace, surrendering up
Thine individual being, shalt thou go
To mix for ever with the elements,
To be a brother to the insensible rock
And to the sluggish clod, which the rude swain
Turns with his share, and treads upon. The oak
Shall send his roots abroad, and pierce thy mould.

Yet not to thine eternal resting-place
Shalt thou return alone, nor couldst thou wish
Couch more magnificent. Thou shalt lie down
With patriarchs of the infant world—with kings,
The powerful of the earth—the wise, the good,
Fair forms, and hoary seers of ages past,
All in one mighty sepulchre. The hills
Rock-ribbed and ancient as the sun,—the vales
Stretching in pensive quietness between;
The venerable woods—rivers that move
In majesty, and the complaining brooks
That make the meadows green; and, poured round all,
Old Ocean's gray and melancholy waste,—
Are but the solemn decorations all
Of the great tomb of man. The golden sun,
The planets, all the infinite host of heaven,
Are shining on the sad abodes of death,
Through the still lapse of ages. All that tread

The globe are but a handful to the tribes
That slumber in its bosom.—Take the wings
Of morning, pierce the Barcan wilderness,
Or lose thyself in the continuous woods
Where rolls the Oregon, and hears no sound,
Save his own dashings—yet the dead are there:
And millions in those solitudes, since first
The flight of years began, have laid them down
In their last sleep—the dead reign there alone.
So shalt thou rest, and what if thou withdraw
In silence from the living, and no friend
Take note of thy departure? All that breathe
Will share thy destiny. The gay will laugh
When thou art gone, the solemn brood of care
Plod on, and each one as before will chase
His favorite phantom; yet all these shall leave
Their mirth and their employments, and shall come
And make their bed with thee. *As the long train*
Of ages glide away, the sons of men,
The youth in life's green spring, and he who goes
In the full strength of years, matron and maid,
The speechless babe, and the gray-headed man—
Shall one by one be gathered to thy side,
By those, who in their turn shall follow them.

So live, that when thy summons comes to join
The innumerable caravan, which moves
To that mysterious realm, where each shall take
His chamber in the silent halls of death,
Thou go not, like the quarry-slave at night,
Scourged to his dungeon, but, sustained and soothed
By an unfaltering trust, approach thy grave,
Like one who wraps the drapery of his couch
About him, and lies down to pleasant dreams.

2. See McDowell, *Bryant,* xxv.

3. Godwin, *Biography,* 1:37.

4. As quoted in Carl Van Doren, "The Growth of Thanatopsis," *Nation* 101 (1915):432.

5. Beilby Porteus, "Death, A Poetical Essay," in *A Summary of Christian Evidences* (Boston, 1814) 133–43.

6. McDowell, *Bryant,* 350. "Not That From Life and All Its Woes" (1815; *North American Review* 1817).

7. "Hymn to Death" (1820; *New York Review,* 1825).

8. McDowell, "Bryant's Practice," *PMLA,* 484.

9. Godwin, *Biography*, 1:37.
10. Van Doren, "Thanatopsis," *Nation*, 432.
11. Ibid., 432.
12. McDowell, *Bryant*, 353–54. "They Taught Me and It was a Fearful Creed" (ca. 1818).
13. Lydia Sigourney, "Versification of a remark by Pliny," *North American Review* 5 (1817):337–38.
14. William Cullen Bryant II, "The Genesis of 'Thanatopsis'," *New England Quarterly* 21 (1948):163–84.
15. Godwin, *Biography*, 1:150.
16. McDowell, "Bryant's Practice," *PMLA*, 482–84.
17. See Grey's "Ode for Music": "The still, small voice of gratitude," and 1 Kings 19:12.
18. See Perry Miller, *The New England Mind: The Seventeenth Century* (Cambridge, Mass.: Harvard University Press, 1954), 331–51.
19. *A Survey of the Summe of Church Discipline* (London, 1648) as quoted in Perry Miller and Thomas H. Johnson, *The Puritan* (New York: American Book, 1938), 65.
20. Arms, "Bryant," *University of Kansas City Review*, 220–22.
21. Elisabeth Kubler-Ross, *On Death and Dying* (New York: MacMillan, 1969), 38–137.
22. "The Burial Place" (1818, *Poems*, 1832).
23. "The Two Graves" (1826; *United States Literary Gazette*, 1826).
24. "Among the Trees" (1868; *Putnam's Magazine*, 1869).
25. "A Lifetime" (1876: *Poetical Works*, 1876).
26. "The Flood of Years" (1876: *Scribner's Monthly*, 1876).

Chapter Four

1. Nevins, *Evening Post*, 135.
2. Bigelow, *Bryant*, 341.
3. Ibid., 340–41.
4. Ibid., 341–42.
5. Ibid., 234.
6. *The Heart of Emerson's Journals*, ed. Bliss Perry (Boston: Houghton Mifflin Co., 1926), 192.
7. Godwin, *Biography*, 1:351.
8. Gordon E. Bigelow, *Rhetoric and American Poetry of the Early National Period*, University of Florida Monographs: Humanities No. 4 (Gainesville: University of Florida Press, 1960), 48–59.
9. *The Embargo*, ed. Thomas O. Mabbott (Gainesville: University of Florida Press, 1955), 37–48.
10. C. I. Glicksberg, "From the 'Pathetic' to the 'Classical': Bryant's

Schooling in the Liberties of Oratory," *American Notes and Queries* 6 (1947):179–82.

11. Author's Note to "The Ages," quoted from *Poetical Works* (1883), 1:335.

12. "The Ages" (1821; *Poems,* 1821).

13. Godwin, *Biography,* 1:171.

14. "The Greek Boy," (1828; *Talisman,* 1829).

15. "The Conjunction of Jupiter and Venus" (1826; *United States Literary Gazette,* 1826).

16. "To the Apennines" (1835; New York *Mirror,* 1835).

17. "The Damsel of Peru" (1826; *United States Review,* 1826).

18. Stanley T. Williams, *The Spanish Background to American Literature* 2 vols. (New Haven: Yale University Press, 1955), 2:129–30.

19. "The Fountain" (1839; *Democratic Review,* 1839).

20. Donald A. Ringe, "William Cullen Bryant and the Science of Geology," *American Literature* 26 (1955):507–14.

21. *Poetical Works,* 1:354–55.

22. "The Antiquity of Freedom" (1842; *Knickerbocker,* 1842).

23. Godwin, *Biography,* 2:188–89.

24. See Aaron Kramer, *The Prophetic Tradition in American Poetry, 1835–1900* (Rutherford, N.J.: Fairleigh Dickinson, 1968), 74.

25. "The Death of Lincoln" (1864; *Atlantic Monthly,* 1865). First titled "Abraham Lincoln, Poetical Tribute to the Memory of Abraham Lincoln" it was later published simply as "Abraham Lincoln" (*Poetical Works,* 1883).

Chapter Five

1. "The Death of Schiller" (1838; *Democratic Review, 1838).*

2. *Letters,* 1:419.

3. Ibid., 3:238.

4. Ibid., 3:305–06.

5. "Letter I. First Impression of an American in France," in McDowell, *Bryant,* 264–67.

6. *Letters,* 2:350.

7. Ibid., 3:243.

8. Ibid., 1:456.

9. Ibid., 3:262.

10. Ibid., 3:467.

11. Ibid., 3:469.

12. Poetical Works (1883), 2:370.

13. Ibid., 2:408.

14. *The Prose Writings of William Cullen Bryant,* ed. Parke Godwin, 2 vols. (New York: D. Appleton & Co., 1884), 1:112–14.

15. Ibid., 1:113–14.
16. Ibid., 1:93–102.
17. "Song" (n.d.; *New York Mirror,* 1835).
18. Williams, *Spanish Background,* 2:146. The attribution of the translation of "Niágra" is also discussed here.
19. *Poems of Uhland,* ed. Waterman T. Hewitt (New York: MacMillan, 1907), 158.
20. "I Think of Thee" (1840; *Godey's Ladies Book,* 1844).
21. "The Saw Mill" (1850; *Graham's Magazine,* 1850).
22. Godwin, *Biography,* 2:193.
23. Quoted in Thomas G. Voss, " 'Not the Highest Praise': A Brief Reintroduction to William Cullen Bryant as a Translator of Homer," in Brodwin, *Centennial Conference,* 201. Much of my discussion is based upon this informative paper.
24. Ibid., 202.
25. Ibid., 201.
26. "The Fifth Book of Homer's Odyssey—Translated" (1871). *Homer: The Odyssey,* trans. Robert Fitzgerald, (Garden City, N.Y.: Anchor Books, Doubleday & Co., 1963), 87. *The Odyssey of Homer,* trans. Richmond Lattimore (New York: Harper & Row, 1965), 94.

Chapter Six

1. *Prose Writings,* 1:15. Arms cites Bryant's "indecisiveness of theory" in "Respectable Station," *University of Kansas City Review,* 218.
2. *Prose Writings,* 1:7–8.
3. Ibid., 1:13.
4. McDowell, *Bryant,* lv–lvi. See also Gay W. Allen, *American Prosody* (New York: American Book Co., 1935), 27–55.
5. *A Library of Poetry and Song,* ed. William Cullen Bryant, (New York: J. B. Ford & Co., 1871), 47–48.
6. Ibid., 48.
7. *Prose Writings,* 1:34.
8. *Library,* 47.
9. *Prose Writings,* 1:6.
10. Ibid., 1:6.
11. Ibid., 1:6.
12. "An Essay on American Poetry," (*North American Review,* 1818), *Prose Writings,* 1:45–56.
13. "The Figure a Poem Makes," preface to *Collected Poems of Robert Frost* (Garden City, N.Y.: Doubleday, 1942), preface.
14. Northrop Frye, *The Anatomy of Criticism* (Princeton, N.J.: Princeton University Press, 1957), 251.
15. "Mutation (1824; *United States Literary Gazette,* 1824).

16. "November" (1824; *United States Literary Gazette,* 1824).
17. "To Cole, the Painter, Departing for Europe" (1829; *Talisman,* 1830).
18. *Prose Writings,* 1:57–67.
19. "In Memoriam" (1856).
20. " 'This do in Remembrance of Me' " (n.d.).
21. "The Death of Channing" (1842).
22. "My Autumn Walk" (1864; *Atlantic Monthly,* 1865).
23. "A Scene on the Banks of the Hudson" (1827; *Talisman,* 1828).
24. "A Lifetime" (1876; *Poetical Works,* 1876).
25. "The Cost of Pleasure" (n.d.).
26. McDowell, "Bryant's Practice," 474–502.
27. Bigelow, *Bryant,* 72–73.
28. *Prose Writings,* 2:17.
29. Ibid., 2:19.
30. Ibid., 2:21.
31. Ibid., 2:150.
32. "A Discourse on the Life, Character and Genius of Washington Irving" (delivered 3 April 1860); in *Prose Writings,* 1:332–67.
33. "Discourse on the Life and Genius of Cooper" (delivered 25 February 1852); in *Prose Writings,* 1:329.
34. Archibald Alison, *Essays on the Nature and Principles of Taste* (Edinborough, 1790).
35. Alison, as quoted in Samuel Monk, *The Sublime* (Ann Arbor: University of Michigan Press, 1960), 148–49.
36. *Prose Writings,* 1:19.
37. "The Painted Cup" (1842; *Democratic Review,* 1842).
38. "Among the Trees" (1868; *Putnam's Magazine,* 1869).

Chapter Seven

1. James T.Fields, *Yesterdays with Authors* (Boston: J. R. Osgood & Co., 1874), as quoted in Leyda, *Melville Log,* 1:384.
2. "Hawthorne and His Mosses," *Literary World* (17 August 1850), as quoted in Leyda, *Melville Log,* 1:389.
3. *Emerson's Journals,* 142.
4. Ibid., 207–08.
5. Ibid., 141.
6. Ibid., 309–10.
7. *Godey's Ladies Book* 30 (April 1846) as reprinted in *The Works of Edgar Allan Poe,* ed. E. C. Stedman and George Woodberry, 6 vols. (New York: Scribner's, 1914) 6:134–35.
8. "My Tribute to Four Poets," in *The Portable Walt Whitman,* ed. Mark Van Doren, Viking Portable Library (New York: Viking Press, 1945)

677. For a perceptive comparison of Bryant and Whitman see Stanley Brodwin, "The 'Denial of Death' in William Cullen Bryant and Walt Whitman," in Brodwin, *Centennial Conference*, 113–31.

9. Harriet Martineau, *Society in America*, 3 vols. (London: Saunders and Otley, 1837) 3:214.

10. James Russell Lowell, *The Complete Poetical Works of James Russell Lowell* (Boston: Houghton, Mifflin Co., 1896), 131–32

11. Bayard Taylor, *The Complete Poetical Works of Bayard Taylor* (Boston: Houghton, Mifflin Co., 1899), 237–40.

12. Niclas Müller, *Neure Lieder and Gedichte* (New York: Nic. Müllers Buckbruckerci, 1867), 13–14.

13. See McDowell, *Bryant*, v; V. L. Parrington, "The Romantic Revolution," in *Main Currents in American Thought* (New York: Harcourt, Brace & Co., 1927), 239.

Selected Bibliography

Primary Sources

The Embargo. Edited by Thomas O. Mabbott. Gainesville: University of Florida Press: Scholars' Facsimiles and Reprints, 1955.
Letters of a Traveler. New York: G.P. Putnam, 1850.
Letters of a Traveler, Second Series. New York: D. Appleton & Co., 1859.
Letters from the East. New York: G. Putnam and Son, 1869.
The Iliad of Homer. Translated into English Blank Verse. 2 vols. Boston: Fields, Osgood & Co., 1870.
The Odyssey of Homer. 2 vols. Boston: James R. Osgood & Co., 1871–72.
The Letters of William Cullen Bryant. Edited by William Cullen Bryant II and Thomas G. Voss. 4 vols. New York: Fordham University Press, 1975–84.
The Poetical Works of William Cullen Bryant. New York: D. Appleton & Co., 1876.
The Poetical Works of William Cullen Bryant. Edited by Parke Godwin. 2 vols. New York: D. Appleton & Co., 1883. (Published as vols. 3 and 4 of *The Life and Writings of William Cullen Bryant.*)
The Prose Writings of William Cullen Bryant. Edited by Parke Godwin. 2 vols. New York: D. Appleton & Co., 1884. (Published as vols. 1 and 2 of *The Life and Writings of William Cullen Bryant.*)

Secondary Sources

Allen, Gay W. "William Cullen Bryant." *American Prosody.* New York: American Book Co., 1935. Full treatment of Bryant's poetic technique.
Arms, George. "William Cullen Bryant: A Respectable Station on Parnassus." *University of Kansas City Review* 15 (1949):215–23. Enlightened, sympathetic treatment of the poet's major achievements.
Bigelow, John. *William Cullen Bryant.* American Men of Letters Series. Boston: Houghton, Mifflin Co., 1890. Outdated account of his public life.
Brodwin, Stanley; D'Innocenzo, Michael; Astman, Joseph G., editors. *William Cullen Bryant and His America: Centennial Conference Proceed-*

ings, 1878–1978. New York: AMS Press, 1983. Papers by leading scholars on Bryant's life and writings.

Brown, Charles H. *William Cullen Bryant.* New York: Scribners, 1971. The authoritative biography, thoroughly researched and documented.

Bryant, William Cullen II. "The Genesis of 'Thanatopsis'." *New England Quarterly* 21 (June 1948): 163–84. Detailed study refuting traditional assumptions about Bryant's early career.

Foerster, Norman. *Nature in American Literature.* Boston: MacMillan, 1923. A useful compilation of recurrent images and themes.

Godwin, Parke, editor. *A Biography of William Cullen Bryant, with extracts from His Private Correspondence.* 2 vols. New York: D. Appleton & Co., 1883. Memoir by his associate, largely supplanted by more recent scholarship.

Jones, Howard M. *Belief and Disbelief in American Literature.* Chicago: University of Chicago Press, 1967. Compares Bryant's religious beliefs with those of Irving and Cooper.

Krapf, Norbert. *Under Open Sky: Poets on William Cullen Bryant.* New York: Fordham University Press, 1986. Contains both short prose pieces and original poems in a striking variety of perceptions of Bryant.

Leonard W. E. "Bryant." *Cambridge History of American Literature,* 1. New York: G. P. Putnam & Sons, 1917. Original and penetrating assessment of the poet and his art.

McDowell, Tremaine. *William Cullen Bryant.* American Writers Series. New York: American Book Co., 1935. Contains a scholarly introduction, representative selections, notes, and a bibliography complete through 1935.

————. "Bryant's Practice in Composition and Revision." *PMLA* 52 (June 1937): 474–502. Thorough study of the early poems based on the original manuscripts.

Nevins, Allan. *The Evening Post: A Century of Journalism.* New York: Boni and Liveright, 1922. Illuminates Bryant's role in journalism and politics.

Parrington, Vernon L. "William Cullen Bryant, Puritan Liberal." *The Romantic Revolution in America.* New York: Harcourt, Brace & Co., 1927. Provocative interpretation of Bryant's political thought; inadequate as literary criticism.

Pattee, F. L. "The Centenary of Bryant's Poetry." *Sidelights on American Literature.* New York: The Century Co., 1922. Balanced, sensitive criticism of thought and poetry.

Peckham, Harry H. *Gotham Yankee.* New York: Vantage Press, 1950. Biography for the casual reader.

Quinn, Arthur H. "The Frontiers of Life and Death." *The Literature of the*

American People. New York: Appleton–Century–Crofts, 1951. Useful summary of biographical information and criticism.

Ringe, Donald A. *Poetry and the Cosmos: William Cullen Bryant.* (unpub. diss.) Harvard University, 1953. Original, thorough study of Bryant's ideas.

—————. "Kindred Spirits: Bryant and Cole." *American Quarterly* 6 (Fall 1954):233–44. Examines the religious and psychological assumptions underlying nature poetry and landscape painting.

Sanford, Charles L. "The Concept of the Sublime in the Works of Thomas Cole and William Cullen Bryant." *American Literature* 28 (January 1957):434–48. A stimulating discussion of romantic aesthetics.

Van Doren, Carl. "The Growth of Thanatopsis." *Nation* 101 (1915):432–33. The first criticism to raise serious questions about this poem.

Index